Frommer's™

Madrid
day BY day™

1st Edition

by Mary-Ann Gallagher

John Wiley & Sons, Ltd

Contents

UK Publisher: Sally Smith
Executive Project Editor: Daniel Mersey
Commissioning Editor: Fiona Quinn
Development Editor: Marcus Waring
Content Editor: Erica Peters
Cartographer: Jeremy Norton
Photo Research: Jill Emeny

Wiley also publishes its books in a variety of electronic formats. Some
content that appears in print may not be available in electronic books.

British Library Cataloguing in Publication Data
A catalogue record for this book is available from the British Library
ISBN: 978-0-470-72172-8
Typeset by Wiley Indianapolis Composition Services
Printed and bound in China by RR Donnelley
5 4 3 2 1

A Note from the Editorial Director

Organizing your time. That's what this guide is all about.

Other guides give you long lists of things to see and do and then expect you to fit the pieces together. The Day by Day guides are different. These guides tell you the best of everything, and then they show you how to see it *in the smartest, most time-efficient way*. Our authors have designed detailed itineraries organized by time, neighborhood, or special interest. And each tour comes with a bulleted map that takes you from stop to stop.

Hoping to visit world-class art museums, be dazzled by the vast Royal Palace, or try superb tapas at traditional taverns? Planning a walk along the Gran Vía, or plotting a day of funfilled activities with the kids? Whatever your interest or schedule, the Day by Days give you the smartest routes to follow. Not only do we take you to the top attractions, hotels, and restaurants, but we also help you access those special moments that locals get to experience— those "finds" that turn tourists into travelers.

The Day by Days are also your top choice if you're looking for one complete guide for all your travel needs. The best hotels and restaurants for every budget, the greatest shopping values, the wildest nightlife—it's all here.

Why should you trust our judgment? Because our authors personally visit each place they write about. They're an independent lot who say what they think and would never include places they wouldn't recommend to their best friends. They're also open to suggestions from readers. If you'd like to contact them, please send your comments our way at feedback@frommers.com, and we'll pass them on.

Enjoy your Day by Day guide—the most helpful travel companion you can buy. And have the trip of a lifetime.

Warm regards,

Kelly Regan

Kelly Regan, Editorial Director
Frommer's Travel Guides

About the Author

Mary-Ann Gallagher is a British travel writer who has spent many years in Spain, and has written dozens of guidebooks for publishers around the world. She now lives in Barcelona with partner Aleix and son Max, but visits the captivating Spanish capital as often as possible.

Acknowledgments

Muchas gracias to Susanna, Eduardo and Max for making Madrid even more fun than usual. Thanks to the press department at the tourist office, the patient museum staff, and all at Frommer's, especially Fiona Quinn for all her hard work, kindness and patience.

An Additional Note

Please be advised that travel information is subject to change at any time—and this is especially true of prices. We therefore suggest that you write or call ahead for confirmation when making your travel plans. The authors, editors, and publisher cannot be held responsible for the experiences of readers while traveling. Your safety is important to us, however, so we encourage you to stay alert and be aware of your surroundings.

Star Ratings, Icons & Abbreviations

Every hotel, restaurant, and attraction listing in this guide has been ranked for quality, value, service, amenities, and special features using a **star-rating system.** Hotels, restaurants, attractions, shopping, and nightlife are rated on a scale of zero stars (recommended) to three stars (exceptional). In addition to the star-rating system, we also use a **kids icon** to point out the best bets for families. Within each tour, we recommend cafes, bars, or restaurants where you can take a break. Each of these stops appears in a shaded box marked with a coffee-cup-shaped bullet ☕ .

The following **abbreviations** are used for credit cards:

AE	American Express	DISC	Discover	V	Visa
DC	Diners Club	MC	MasterCard		

Frommers.com

Now that you have this guidebook to help you plan a great trip, visit our website at **www.frommers.com** for additional travel information on more than 4,000 destinations. We update features regularly to give you instant access to the most current trip-planning information available. At Frommers. com, you'll find scoops on the best airfares, lodging rates, and car rental bargains. You can even book your travel online through our reliable travel booking partners.

A Note on Prices

In the "Take a Break" and "Best Bets" sections of this book, we have used a system of dollar signs to show a range of costs for 1 night in a hotel (the price of a double-occupancy room) or the cost of an entree at a restaurant. Use the following table to decipher the dollar signs:

Cost	Hotels	Restaurants
$	under $100	under $10
$$	$100–$200	$10–$20
$$$	$200–$300	$20–$30
$$$$	$300–$400	$30–$40
$$$$$	over $400	over $40

An Invitation to the Reader

In researching this book, we discovered many wonderful places—hotels, restaurants, shops, and more. We're sure you'll find others. Please tell us about them, so we can share the information with your fellow travelers in upcoming editions. If you were disappointed with a recommendation, we'd love to know that, too. Please write to:

Frommer's Madrid, Day by Day, 1st Edition
Wiley Publishing, Inc. • 111 River St. • Hoboken, NJ 07030-5774

12 Favorite
Moments

12 Favorite Moments

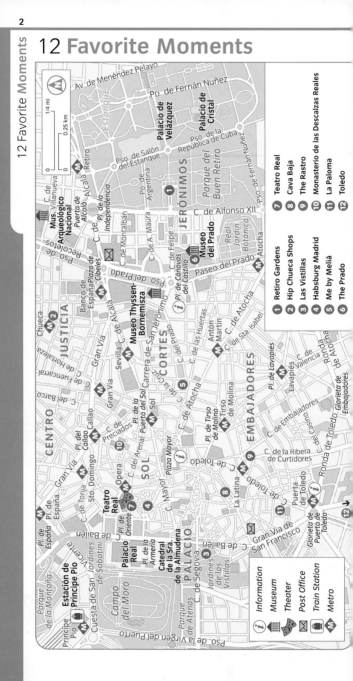

1 Retiro Gardens
2 Hip Chueca Shops
3 Las Vistillas
4 Habsburg Madrid
5 Me by Meliá
6 The Prado
7 Teatro Real
8 Cava Baja
9 The Rastro
10 Monasterio de las Descalzas Reales
11 La Paloma
12 Toledo

Information
Museum
Theater
Post Office
Train Station
Metro

1/4 mi
0.25 km

No European capital can compare with Madrid when it comes to showing visitors a good time. The city boasts three of the world's best art museums, magnificent royal monuments, smart shops, glorious gardens, and hundreds of fabulous tapas bars and restaurants. At its heart is the beautifully preserved old quarter, which hums with life day and night.

❶ Lazing in the Retiro Gardens. Madrid's beautiful public park is a green expanse full of shady pathways, fountains, and dainty pavilions. I come with my son to feed the carp at the boating lake, and then enjoy a picnic under the trees. *See p 92.*

❷ Shopping in Chueca's quirky boutiques. The smart shops of Salamanca are more famous, but I prefer to amble around the little boutiques of boho-chic Chueca. *See p 60.*

❸ Watching the sun set over the Sierras. I love to sit at a terrace café in Las Vistillas and watch the sun sink behind the distant mountains and set the Madrid sky on fire. As night falls, the Royal Palace is theatrically silhouetted against the stars. *See p 89.*

Enjoy a lazy day in Retiro Gardens.

❹ Getting lost in Habsburg Madrid. History oozes from every stone in the heart of Habsburg Madrid. The web of narrow streets and enchanting squares around the showcase Plaza Mayor has changed surprisingly little since the 16th century. *See p 39.*

❺ Sipping cocktails at a hip rooftop bar. Once the heat of summer kicks in, everyone flocks to the *terrazas* (outdoor bars). Best of these are the fashionable new rooftop bars at some of the city's hottest hotels, including the Hotel De Las Letras, the Penthouse at the über-cool Me by Meliá, or La Terraza at every fashionista's favorite, the Urban. Dressing up, relaxing with a cocktail, and watching the city sparkling at my feet has to be one of my favorite Madrid experiences. *See p 109.*

❻ Gazing at the masterworks of the Paseo del Arte. Madrid's three great art museums—the Prado, the Thyssen, and the Reina Sofía—are among the finest anywhere in the world. From the Italian primitives in the Thyssen or the masterpieces by Velázquez in the Prado, to the latest contemporary creations at the Reina Sofía, the capital has it all. *See p 28.*

❼ Enjoying a night at the opera. The opulent opera house is a whirl of red velvet and gilt, and many Madrileños still wear evening dress to attend the opera. It's perfect for a romantic night out. *See p 123.*

8 Tapas-bar hopping. Madrid's tapas bars range from spit-and-sawdust dives that have barely changed in decades, to swish gourmet establishments serving fashionable wines and elegant nibbles. Eating and drinking my way around the city is an utter joy. *See p 52.*

9 Rummaging for bargains in the Rastro. I am a flea market addict, but few can compare with Madrid's Rastro for sheer scale and exuberance. The range is astonishing—from traditional leather goods to car parts. The obligatory post-Rastro bar crawl around the tapas bars of La Latina is just as much fun as exploring the market itself. *See p 77.*

10 Touring royal convents for blue-blooded nuns. Madrid has two historic convents for aristocratic nuns. I love visiting the gruesome Reliquary room at the Monasterio de la Encarnación, full of extraordinary receptacles containing the bones, limbs, teeth, and hair of the saints and martyrs. At the Monasterio de las Descalzas Reales, I particularly enjoy the exquisite cloister. *See p 14.*

11 Joining in a popular street festival. During the summer, the city explodes with a series of colorful, traditional festivals, which take place in different neighborhoods, usually in honor of the patron saint, San Isidro. The biggest are the Fiestas de San Isidro in May, but each festival offers visitors a chance to join in with traditional events from parades to street parties. *See p 158.*

12 Exploring the ancient streets of historic Toledo. I really enjoy escaping to the beautiful old city of Toledo, losing myself in its lovely streets and quiet corners. It's much more enjoyable to stay the night, when the city magically empties of day-trippers. *See p 152.* ●

Fans for sale at Rastro Market.

The Best **in One Day**

Information
Theater
Post Office
Rail Station
Metro

1 Plaza Mayor
2 Museo del Prado
3 Parque del Retiro
4 La Mallorquina
5 Museo Thyssen-Bornemisza
6 Centre de Arte Reina Sofia
7 Arola Madrid
8 Plaza de Oriente
9 Palacio Real
10 Catedral de la Almudena
11 Jardines de las Vistillas
12 Restaurante El Ventorrillo

This full and art-intensive day takes in Madrid's trio of superb art museums, the Prado, the Reina Sofía, and the Thyssen-Bornemisza, but also includes ample recovery time in two magnificent squares and the glorious Parque del Retiro. It ends with a visit to the opulent Royal Palace. START: **Metro to Sol.**

1 ★★★ Plaza Mayor. The vast pedestrian Plaza Mayor, enclosed by ranks of gleaming mansions and accessed by nine massive archways, is classic Habsburg. The site of hangings, bullfights, royal ceremonies, festivals, and the macabre *autos da fé* (the Inquisition executions), it became the city's main square under Felipe II in the late 16th century, when the Royal Court finally settled in Madrid and made it the capital. Order a coffee from one of the cafés with outdoor tables and soak up the history. See also p 39. ⏲ *45 min. Metro: Sol.*

2 ★★★ Museo del Prado. This is one of the world's greatest art museums, originally assembled by the Habsburg kings. To see it properly would take days, but visiting just one gallery (Room 12, First Floor of the main Villanueva building) will give you a taster. This huge

Soak up at the history at Plaza Mayor.

octagonal room contains works by the greatest artist of the Spanish Golden Age, Diego Velázquez (1599–1660). One painting stands out: *Las Meninas* (1656) depicts the 4-year-old Infanta Margarita and her entourage, with Velázquez himself gazing out from behind his easel. Look beyond the apparently simple court scene and its complexity and elusiveness grows. See also the Prado tour, p 24. ⏲ *1 hr. Paseo del Prado s/n.* ☎ *91-330-28-00, or* ☎ *902-10-70-77. www.museodel prado.es. Admission 6€ adults, 3€ students, free for under-18s when bought directly at ticket office; available in advance for 9€ adults, free for under-6s; also part of the Paseo del Arte ticket 14.40€. Tues–Sat 9am–8pm, Dec 24, Dec 31, 6 Jan 9am–2pm. Closed Mon, Dec 25, Jan 1, Good Friday, May 1. Audioguide available for permanent collection 3.50€, temporary exhibition 3.50€, or both 5€. Metro: Banco de España.*

3 ★★★ kids Parque del Retiro. After the fascinating but overwhelming Prado, the magnificent Retiro Park is close by. Here children can frolic in the playgrounds by the Calle Alcalá entrance or kick a ball around on the lawns. The elegantly arranged Parterre gardens are restful, while the enormous Estanque (lake) with its marble colonnade hints that it was once a royal garden attached to the long-demolished palace of Buen Retiro. Now teeming with plump koi carp, the lake is filled with bobbing boats that can be rented by the hour. The atmosphere is carnivalesque, with mime artists, buskers, ice-cream vendors and snack kiosks, and cheerful crowds. It's a great place for a picnic, and, even on the hottest day, you can always find a shady corner. Head down to the pool near the beautiful Palacio de Cristal. For more on the highlights of the park, see Parque del Retiro, p 92. *1 hr. Entrances on Cl Alcalá, Cl Alfonso XII, Av. Menéndez Pelayo, Paseo de Reina Cristina. Daily May–Sept 6am–midnight, Oct 6am–11pm, Nov–Apr 6am–10pm. Metro: Retiro.*

Parque del Retiro sculpture.

🍴 **★★ La Mallorquina.** There are kiosks in the park for a quick bite, but for an upmarket picnic head one block up Calle Serrano from the park entrance by Puerta de Alcalá to find La Mallorquina. They have the best take-out sandwiches, pies, cakes, and pastries in town. *C/Serrano 6–8. ☎ 91-577-18-59. $–$$.*

⑤ ★★★ Museo Thyssen-Bornemisza. Across from the Prado, the elegant, neoclassical Palacio de Villahermosa is now home to the vast Thyssen-Bornemisza collection, acquired by the Baron Van Thyssen and his ex-Miss Spain wife, Carmen Cervera. Again, choosing just one section to highlight, the Impressionists (Gallery 32, First Floor) seem fitting after the Retiro park. Claude Monet's dreamy *The Thaw in Vétheuil* (1881), and his celebrated *Charing Cross Bridge*, barely visible in a white fog, are my favorites. In the adjoining gallery (33) are Degas' *Swaying Dancer* (1877–9) and Cézanne's dapper *Portrait of a Farmer* (1905–6). See also the tour of the highlights of the Thyssen-Bornemisza, p 30. *1 hr. Paseo del Prado 8. ☎ 91-369-01-51. www.museothyssen.org. Admission to permanent collection 6€ adults, 4€ students, free for under-12s; temporary exhibition prices vary. Combined*

Museo del Prado is one of the world's greatest art museums.

Paseo del Arte Discounts: With a single ticket, the Tarjeta Paseo del Arte, you can visit the Prado, the Thyssen-Bornemisza, and the Reina Sofía. Buy it at museum ticket offices (14.40€).

Madrid Card: The Madrid Card, available for 24, 48, or 72 hours, offers admission to more than 40 museums (including the three big Paseo del Arte museums), major attractions including the zoo, fun-fair, and Bernabéu football stadium, and unlimited use of the Madrid Visión Tour bus. It can be supplemented with the Tourist Travel Pass (abono turístico), which offers unlimited use of the public transport system for 1, 2, 3, 4, 5, or 7 days (5–22.60€ for central Madrid, or 9–45€ for Madrid plus outlying towns including Toledo and Aranjuez). More information at www.madridcard.com.

admission to permanent and temporary collection available. Also part of Paseo del Arte ticket, 14.40€. Tues–Sun 10am–7pm, ticket office closes 6.30pm. Closed Mon, Dec 25, Jan 1, May 1. Audioguide available to permanent and temporary collections. Metro: Banco de España.

6 ★★★ Centre de Arte Reina Sofía. The fashionable Reina Sofía is the city's modern art museum. It is also home (Gallery 7, Second Floor) to Picasso's masterpiece *Guernica* (1937), painted in memory of the brutal bombing of an ancient Basque town by the Germans with Franco's approval in 1937. See also the tour of the highlights of the Reina Sofía, p 32. ⏱ *1 hr. Cl Santa Isabel 52.* ☎ *91-774-10-00. www.museureina sofia.es. Admission to permanent collection 6€ adults, 3€ students, free for under-12s; temporary exhibition prices vary. Combined admission to permanent and temporary collection available. Also part of Paseo del Arte ticket, 14.40€. Mon, Wed–Sun 10am–9pm, ticket office closes 6.30pm. Closed Tues, Dec 24, Dec 25, Dec 31, Jan 1, Jan 6, May 1, May 15, Sept 7, Free Sat 2.30–9pm, Sun 10am–2.30pm, May 18, Oct 12, Dec 6.*

Audioguide available to permanent and temporary collections. Guided visits in Spanish only Mon and Wed 5pm, Sat 11pm. Metro: Banco de España.

7 ★ Arola Madrid. If you're gasping for a sit-down, try this stylish new café in the striking extension to the Reina Sofía. The huge curving red walls remind me of a spaceship, and the excellent coffee, sandwiches, and pastries will restore you. See p100. *Cl Argumosa 43.* ☎ *91-467-02-02. $$.*

Centre de Arte Reina Sofía.

8 ★★ kids **Plaza de Oriente.**
Jump on the efficient metro at
Atocha, with a quick change at Sol,
to emerge at Ópera. Walk around to
the front of the lavish Opera House
to find the impressive Plaza de Oriente. With the enormous Royal
Palace, the Opera House, and neat
gardens with fountains and statues,
this is the city's grandest square.
After a short stroll around the gardens (there's a playground for
youngsters), treat yourself to an ice
cream and grandstand views at one
of the smart café terraces. ⏲ *30
min. Metro: Ópera.*

9 ★★★ kids **Palacio Real.** Prepare yourself for an assault on the
Royal Palace, an immense 18th-cen-
tury construction that has almost
3,000 rooms. Fortunately, just a
handful are open to the public.
Leave the lavish interior for another
day, and explore the expansive main
courtyard and the two small museums just off it. These contain a
charming old pharmacy and the
interesting Royal Armory, with

extravagant suits of armor for men
and mounts. I like the exquisitely
engraved armor used by Charles V
(Carlos I of Spain) in the Battle of
Mühlberg (1547). See also the tour
of Old Madrid, p35. ⏲ *1½ hrs. Cl
Bailén.* ☎ *91-454-87-00. Admission
to Palace, Pharmacy, and Royal
Armory with guided visit: 10€
adults, 6€ students and children
5–16, or 8€ without guide, no concessions; guided visit to Palace,
Pharmacy, Royal Armory, and Picture Gallery: 11€ adults, 7€ students and children 5–16. Picture
gallery only 2€, no concessions;
Royal Armory only 3.40€ adults,
2.50€ students and children 5–16,
free non-guided visits for EU-citizens
Wed (take your passport). Oct–Mar
Mon–Sat 9.30am–5pm, Sun
9.30am–2pm; Apr–Sept Mon–Sat
9am–6pm, Sun 9am–3pm. Closed
Jan 1, Jan 7, May 1, Sept 9, Oct 12,
Dec 24, Dec 25, Dec 31. Metro:
Ópera.*

10 ★ **Catedral de la Almudena.** From the Royal Palace, walk

Take a stroll around the grand Plaza de Oriente.

The immense 18th-century Palacio Real.

south down the busy Calle Bailén. On the right soars the massive cathedral. Peep in to see the lovely stained glass windows, which fill the cavernous interior with jewel-colored light, and the statue of La Virgen de la Almudena, the city's patron saint. According to legend, she is credited with ensuring that the Moors were ousted during the time of the Reconquest. ⏱ *20 min. Free. Daily 10am–7.30pm, no entry to tourists during mass. Metro: Ópera.*

⑪ ★★ **Jardines de las Vistillas.** These small gardens, unfortunately rather shabby, are at the center of a buzzy bar and restaurant district, which has sprung up because of the glorious views of the distant sierras. Ignore the gardens and head for the bars and their terraces. The district faces west, and the sight of the setting sun turning the sky scarlet behind the grand silhouettes of the cathedral and the Royal Palace is breathtaking. ⏱ *45 min. Metro: La Latina.*

🍵 ★★ **Restaurante El Ventorillo.** Pull up a chair on the terrace of this old-fashioned restaurant and join the Madrileños watching the sunset. The restaurant has good house wines, beers, and a wide range of tapas. The main dishes are slightly pricey but the setting is unforgettable. *Cl De Bailén 14.* ☎ *91-366-35-78. $$.*

Catedral de la Almudena.

The Best **Full-Day Tours**

The Best **in Two Days**

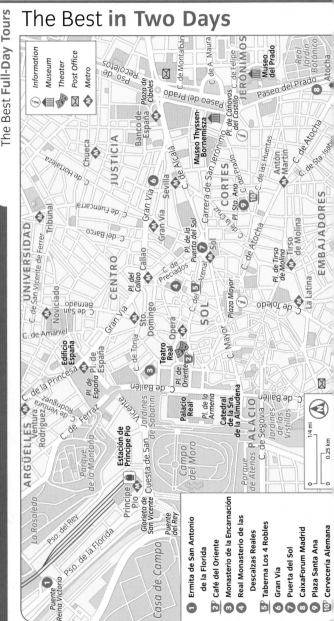

Information
Museum
Theater
Post Office
Metro

1 Ermita de San Antonio
   de la Florida
2 Café del Oriente
3 Monasterio de la Encarnación
4 Real Monasterio de las
   Descalzas Reales
5 Taberna Los 4 Robles
6 Gran Vía
7 Puerta del Sol
8 CaixaForum Madrid
9 Plaza Santa Ana
10 Cervecería Alemana

With Madrid's blockbuster sights under your belt, a more leisurely pace is in order on your second day. This itinerary takes in some of the quirkier attractions, including a convent for blue-blooded nuns, an extraordinary cabinet of reliquaries, and the tomb of that most Madrileño of painters, Goya. And there is a dash of contemporary pizzazz with the city's showcase shopping street, the Gran Vía. START: **Metro to Ópera.**

① ★★ **Ermita de San Antonio de la Florida.** This small chapel may seem off the beaten track, but it's just a short one-stop ride from the Ópera metro. A neoclassical jewel, it is now most famous for its vivid and charming frescoes, painted by the finest Spanish artist of the late 18th and early 19th centuries, Francisco de Goya (1746–1828). Goya died in Bordeaux, France, but his remains were brought back to this chapel in 1919. His recently restored frescoes occupy the entire cupola and glow with life and color. They depict St Anthony raising a murdered man to life in order to exonerate the saint's father, who stood accused of the crime. Instead of a heavenly host surrounding the saint, Goya painted in a balcony and filled it with contemporary Madrileños, particularly the *majos* and *majas*, (the swaggering dandies of the working class), who were his favorite subject. The painting is transformed from a dull religious work into an engaging and witty evocation of the city. Visit June 9 to 13, when the chapel is the center of a lively festival in honor of the saint, with street fairs, parades, and traditional dancing. ⏱ *45 min. Glorieta de San Antonio de la Florida 5.* ☎ *91-542-07-22. www.munimadrid. es/ermita. Admission free. Sept–July Tues–Fri 9.30am–8pm, Sat–Sun 10am–2pm. Aug Tues–Fri 9.30am–2.30pm, Sat–Sun 10am–2pm. Closed Jan 1, May 1, Sept 9, Dec 24, Dec 25, Dec 31. Metro: Príncipe Pío.*

② ★★★ **Café del Oriente.** This may be one of the more touristy cafés, but it's still one of the best. Its elegant gilded salons are popular with well-heeled ladies and their lapdogs, but the fantastic terrace overlooking Madrid's most regal square is the place to sit. Perfect for a leisurely breakfast, while you admire the views of the gardens, fountains, and splendid Royal Palace. *Plaza de Oriente 2.* ☎ *91-541-39-74. $.*

Monasterio de la Encarnación.

3 ★★ **kids** **Monasterio de la Encarnación.** This austerely beautiful convent was established in 1611 by Margarita of Austria, wife of Felipe III. It is still home to a closed community of nuns, but visits are possible with a guide. The countless treasures, which the convent acquired thanks to its royal patron, have long been dispersed, but the lack of riches amplifies the sublime qualities of this restrained Baroque building. There is one great treasure, among the strangest in Madrid: the relic room. In this thrillingly macabre chamber, more than 4,000 reliquaries, containing the bones, hair, teeth, and limbs of saints and martyrs, line every wall. Foremost among them is the blood of San Pantaleón, which is said to liquefy every year on July 2. If it happens at any other time, so legend goes, the city is in danger. See also p 37. ⏱ *1 hr. Plaza de la Encarnación 1.* ☎ *91-454-88-00. www.patrimonio nacional.es. Admission 3.60€ adults, 2.90€ students and children 5–16, free Wed for EU-citizens; combined admission ticket with Monasterio de Las Descalzas Reales 6€ adults,*

4.90€ students and children 5–16. June–Sept Tues–Sat 10am–8pm; Tues, Wed, Thurs, Sat 10.30am–12.45pm and 4–5.45pm, Fri 10.30am–12.45pm, Sun and public hols 11am–1.45pm Sun 10am–3pm. Closed Jan 1, Easter weekend, May 1, May 15, Sept 9, Dec 24, Dec 25, Dec 31. Metro: Ópera.

4 **kids** **Real Monasterio de las Descalzas Reales.** This translates as the Royal Monastery of Barefoot Royals, but there is nothing ascetic about it. Established for blue-blooded nuns, this is opulent where the Encarnación convent is restrained, and has managed to retain important works of art, including a magnificent series of tapestries by Rubens. Founded in 1559 by the king's sister, Juana of Austria, it occupies a striking baroque building in the city center. There is still a small community of nuns here too, and the convent is only open for guided tours. For highlights, see p 38. ⏱ *1 hr. Plaza de las Descalzas s/n.* ☎ *91-454-88-00. www.patrimonionacional.es. Admission 5€ adults, 4€ students and children 5–16, free Wed to*

Real Monasterio de las Descalzas Reales.

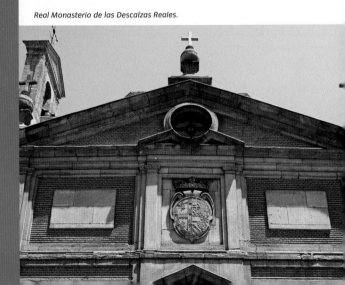

Gran Via, linking the city from east to west.

EU-citizens; combined admission ticket with Real Monasterio de la Encarnación 6€, students and children 5–16 4.90€. June–Sept Tues–Sat 10am–8pm, Sun 10am–3pm; Oct–May Tues; Wed, Thurs and Sat 10.30am–12.45pm and 4–5.45pm. Fri 10.30am–12.45pm, Sun and public hols 11am–1.45pm. Closed Jan 1, Easter weekend, May 1, May 15, Sept 9, Dec 24, Dec 25, Dec 31. Metro: Sol.

5 ★★★ Taberna Los 4 Robles. This cheerfully old-fashioned tavern is handily located just around the corner from the Monasterio de las Descalzas Reales. Brightly lit and decorated with colorful tiles, it's a great place to refuel with coffee or a beer and some tapas—see what's chalked up on the board before choosing. Join the locals at the bar, and toss your used napkins on the floor in true Spanish fashion. *Plaza Celenque 1.* ☎ *91-522-76-86. $.*

6 ★★ Gran Vía. Two convents, however fascinating, is enough for one day. The Gran Vía is known, with more bravura than truth, as the *Broadway Madrileño* for its concentration of musical theaters.

Laid out in the early 20th-century, this long, broad avenue cuts straight across the city, linking east to west. Designed to show the world that Madrid was no backwater sunk in the past, it is lined with outrageously pompous buildings in a mish-mash of once-fashionable styles—lavish neoclassical, sleek Art Deco, and twirling Art Nouveau, all built on a monumental scale. There is certainly a hint of the great avenues of New York, Chicago, or even some South American capitals—despite the best efforts of the international fast food chains to make all city streets look the same around the world. Look up to note the architecture, because at street level, your gaze will no doubt be diverted by the shop windows. Every major Spanish chain can be found here, including some great bookshops such as the Casa del Libro (No. 29), the fashion phenomenon Zara (No. 32), and plenty more. The Gran Vía is at its best in the late afternoon, with the sun setting and the neon signs glowing against the buildings. ⏱ *1 hr. Metro: Gran Vía, Callao and Plaza de España.*

7 ★★ Puerta del Sol. You will no doubt find yourself at the Puerta

King Carlos III in Puerta del Sol.

del Sol several times during your visit, however brief. It's the city's main transport hub, and the confluence of numerous metro and bus routes. Once this was one of the most piquant squares in the city, where anything and anyone was available for a price. Now, it's frankly rather dull, exacerbated by the immense hoardings protecting the works going on beneath the surface to bring local trains into the area as well. Still, it's worth a quick visit to check out Kilómetro Cero—the very center of Spain, which is marked on

a plaque in front of the Casa de Correos (the ochre-colored 18th-century building bristling with flags). If you're in Madrid on New Year's Eve, this is the place to come, armed with a bottle of cava and 12 grapes (one for each chime during the countdown to midnight). ⏱ *20 min. Metro: Sol.*

⑧ ★★ kids **CaixaForum Madrid.** Back on the Paseo del Arte, opposite the Prado, is the city's newest art institution, the Caixa-Forum, which opened in 2007. Get a program in advance from the tourist office: all kinds of great activities are on offer, from art exhibitions and concerts to family days and special activities for children. The building itself is a stunning contemporary conversion of an 1899 power station, topped with a two-floor annex enclosed by a bold rusted iron sculpture. Inside you find a decent café-restaurant (with windows peeking through the mottled iron) and a good book and gift-shop. Best of all is the Vertical Garden, by French botanic artist Patrick Blanc, an enormous wall covered with more than 200 plant species in intricate

CaixaForum, the city's newest art institution.

There are many terrace cafés on Plaza Santa Ana.

designs. It's my favorite piece of public art in the city. ⏺ *1 hr. Paseo del Prado 36.* ☎ *91-330-73-00. www. lacaixa.es/obrasocial. Admission varies according to exhibition and activity, but most are free. Tues–Sun 10am–8pm. Metro: Atocha.*

9 ★ **kids Plaza Santa Ana.** The Plaza Santa Ana is the main hub of the Barrio de las Letras (see tour p 56), the old stomping ground of writers such as Cervantes, Quevado, and Lope de Vega, and more recently, Ernest Hemingway and Nobel-prize-winning writer Jacinto Benavente. The square is crammed on every side with great cafés, bars, and restaurants, all overlooked at one end by the very stylish Me By Meliá hotel, which occupies a turn-of-the-20th-century wedding cake of a building, and at the other by the neoclassical Teatro Espanol, which stands on the site of one of the city's first purpose-built theaters. There are numerous terraces to sit outside and enjoy a beer. It's popular in the afternoons with young local families, thanks to the play areas. Even more bars, cafés, and clubs can be found in the network of streets leading off the square, making it one of the most popular nightlife zones in the city. I avoid it at weekends, when it gets too crowded, and enjoy it best early in the evening during the week. ⏺ *1 hr. Metro: Sol.*

10 ★ **Cerveceria Alemana.** Yet another of Hemingway's haunts, this celebrated tavern retains its original wooden façade, draped lace curtains, and scuttling, long-aproned waiters. Traditional tapas such as *croquetas*, tortilla, and fried fish are accompanied by a wide range of local and international beers. I like it best in winter, when the wood-paneled bar feels especially cozy. *Plaza Santa Ana.* ☎ *91-429-70-33. $.*

Fresh seafood at Hemingway's old haunt, the Alemana.

The Best **in Three Days**

Legend:
- † Church
- ◈ Metro

1 Museo Arqueológico Nacional
2 Calle Serrano
3 Jardines del Descubrimiento
4 Museo Lázaro Galdiano
5 Teatriz
6 Templo de Debod
7 Parque del Oeste
8 La Casa del Chocolate de Tino Helguera
9 Teleférico
10 Casa del Campo
11 Entrevinos

After a culture-packed morning in the chi chi *barrio* of Salamanca (with some shopping as respite from the museums), your third day tour heads to the gardens of northeast Madrid to gaze at an Egyptian temple and catch a cable car to the city's biggest park: the fun-filled Casa de Campo. START: **Metro to Serrano.**

1 ★★★ Museo Arqueológico Nacional. Until 2011, Spain's largest and most important archaeological museum is showing only its highlights while major remodeling works are completed. Among the 268 outstanding pieces are ancient Iberian sculptures, including the mysterious Dama de Elche, a 4th-century bust of a woman in an elaborate headdress. Also seek out the Treasure of Guarrazar, a glittering hoard of Byzantine-style crowns, crosses, and liturgical objects that date back to the time of the Visigoths. I particularly love the Paleolithic art found in the ancient caves of northern Spain, such as the deer bone exquisitely etched with a hunting scene. ⏱ *1 hr. Cl Serrano 13.* ☎ *91-577-79-12. http://man.mcu.es. Admission free. Tues–Sat 9.30am– 8pm, Sun 9.30am–3pm. Closed Jan 1, Jan 6, May 1, Sept 9, Dec 24, Dec 25, Dec 31. Metro: Serrano.*

2 ★ Shopping along Calle Serrano. Calle Serrano is the smartest shopping street in town, traversing the upmarket neighborhood of Salamanca. All the designer names are here, from Spanish luxury goods store Loewe (No. 26) to Gucci (No. 49). Once a favorite street with Victoria Beckham while her husband David was playing with Real Madrid soccer club, it's common to see 'It-girls' and celebrities with oversized sunglasses and undersized dogs. Even if you're on a budget the window-shopping is enjoyable. Musgo (No. 18) has an inexpensive and colorful selection of items for the home, accessories, and gifts. For a traditional deli, try Mantequerías Bravo, just off Serrano at Calle Ayala 24. One-stop shoppers should head to the dependable Spanish department store, El Corte Inglés (No. 47), or the plush ABC Serrano mall, in an attractively tiled former newspaper office (No. 61). ⏱ *1 hr. Cl Serrano. Metro: Serrano or Retiro.*

Ancient Byzantine-style treasures can be found in the Museo Arqueológico Nacional.

Calle Serrano, the smartest shopping street in town.

③ kids Jardines del Descubrimiento. The Gardens of Discovery, next to the archaeological museum, commemorate Columbus's voyage to the Americas in 1492. In one corner, an elaborate 19th-century statue of the explorer stands high on a pedestal, while across the square is a huge sculpture by Vaquero Turcios dedicated to the Discovery of America. In summer, the shady groves of olive and pine trees are the perfect retreat. ⏲ *30 min. Entrances on Calle Serrano and Paseo de la Castellana. Metro: Serrano or Colón.*

④ ★★ Museo Lázaro Galdiano. A private museum in a handsome neo-Renaissance mansion, this varied collection was acquired by Lázaro Galdiano, a wealthy financier. It includes paintings, sculpture, ceramics, coins, furniture, textiles, and clocks. See the Cámara del Tesoro ('Treasure Chamber'), with an assortment of reliquaries and antique glassware. Among the paintings are works by Velázquez, Zurbarán, and Goya (First Floor galleries). ⏲ *1 hr. C/Serrano 122.* ☎ *91-560-60-84. www.flg. es. Admission free Sun, 4€ Mon–Sat adults, 2€ senior citizens & students, free under 12s accompanied by adult. Wed-Mon 10am–4.30pm. Closed public hols. Metro: Rubén Darío.*

⑤ ★ Teatriz. Designed by übercool Philippe Starck in the 1980s, Teatriz remains a favorite with Madrid's *gente guapa* (beautiful people). Some of the original details of the historic theater have been retained, and blue-and-silver fountains add contemporary glamour. Modern Italian cuisine, with lighter fare by the bar. *Cl Hermosilla 15.* ☎ *91-577-53-79. $$$.*

⑥ ★★ kids Templo de Debod. Head across town on the metro to emerge at the Plaza de España.

Visit Lázaro Galdiano's varied art collection.

The Templo de Debod originally stood on the banks of the Nile.

Walk north up Calle Ferraz to find the Templo de Debod, which emerges like a mirage from a pool in the Parque del Oeste. This 4th-century BC Ptolemaic temple was given to the Spanish government in 1968 as a gift for preserving Egyptian monuments threatened by the construction of the Aswan Dam. It originally stood on the banks of the Nile. Inside a small exhibition relates the temple's history, but it's at its most dramatic outside at dusk, when it is beautifully reflected in the shimmering pool. ⏱ *1 hr. Cl Ferraz 1.* ☎ *91-366-74-15. Admission free. Oct–Mar Tues–Fri 9.45am–1.45pm, 4.15–6.15pm, Sat–Sun 10am–2pm; Apr–Sept Tues–Fri 10am–2pm, 6–8pm, Sat–Sun 10am–2pm. Free guided visits for families (in Spanish) first Sat of every month (except Aug) at 11.30am and 12.30pm. Metro Plaza de España or Ventura Rodríguez.*

7 ★★★ kids **Parque del Oeste.** This leafy, green park is a welcome retreat from the searing summer heat. Find a quiet corner under the mature trees and gaze at the distant Sierra de Guadarrama. Younger children enjoy the small play park near the cable-car entrance. The adjacent Paseo Pintor Rosales is lined with cafés, bars, and restaurants where people flock on hot days or nights to enjoy the breezy terraces. The park also boasts a beautiful rose garden,

La Rosaleda, with fountains and a sea of multi-colored blooms. Come in May, during the annual International Roses Competition, to see it at its finest. On a more somber note, this hillside contains the communal grave of the Madrileños shot on May 3, 1808, when Napoleon's troops invaded the city. (This scene is depicted by Goya in his dark painting *El Tres de Mayo 1808,* which hangs in the Prado.) A monument next to the cable car station marks the spot. ⏱ *1 hr. Entrances on Cl Ruperto Chapi, Avda Arco Victoria. Always open. Metro: Plaza de España, Moncloa, or Príncipe Pío.*

8 ★ kids **La Casa del Chocolate de Tino Helguera.** Not only does this shop-cum-tearoom make delicious hot chocolate, but the handmade chocolates (served at the Prince of Asturias's wedding) are heavenly as well. My favorites are the white chocolates with pear and ginger. *Cl Ferraz 30.* ☎ *91-541-28-15. $$.*

9 ★★★ kids **Teleférico.** In the center of the Parque del Oeste, the cable-car station transports you across to the vast wilderness of the Casa del Campo. The cable car sways about 40m (122 feet) in the air, for almost 2½km. Children love it, but those afraid of heights might

The beautiful rose garden in Parque del Oeste.

not. Along the way, you can admire the pretty dome of Goya's burial chapel (see p 13). The cable car arrives at a little café-bar in the center of the Casa del Campo, from where you can walk to the park's biggest attractions: the funfair, the zoo (see p 51), and the lake. There are no signposts but you will see the tall plume of water at the center of the lake in one direction, and the rollercoaster of the funfair in the other. The zoo is just beyond the funfair. They look farther away than they are but are all within 10 or 15 minutes' walk. ⏱ *30 min. Paseo del Pintor Rosales s/n.* ☎ *91-541-11-18. www.teleferico.com. Opening hours vary considerably, but are generally weekends only in winter, summer Mon–Fri 12–1.15pm, 3.15–9pm, Sat–Sun 12–9pm, Check full timetable online or at the tourist office. Metro: Argüelles.*

⑩ ★★ kids Boating in the Casa del Campo. The park information office for the Casa del Campo is next to the lake. You can also rent out rowing boats—one of my favorite things to do on hot days. The spray from the enormous jet of water at the center of the lake is delightfully refreshing. ⏱ *1–2 hrs. Park information office next to lake.* ☎ *91-479-60-02. Info office open May–Sept 15 Tues–Sun and public hols 10am–2pm, 5–8pm. Park always open. Metro: Batán or Lago. Cable car from Paseo del Pintor Rosales s/n. Bus 31, 33, 36, 39, 65, 138 to/from lake. Bus 33 to/from zoo and Parque de Atracciones.*

⑪ ★ Entrevinos. One of the best wine bars in the city, Entrevinos is within staggering distance of the *teleférico* (cable car) station in the Parque del Oeste, and the perfect retreat after all the fun in the park. Laidback and mellow, it offers an astonishing selection of wines (including at least a dozen by the glass) accompanied by excellent gourmet tapas. *Cl Ferraz 36.* ☎ *91-548-31-14. $$.* ●

The Highlights **of the Prado**

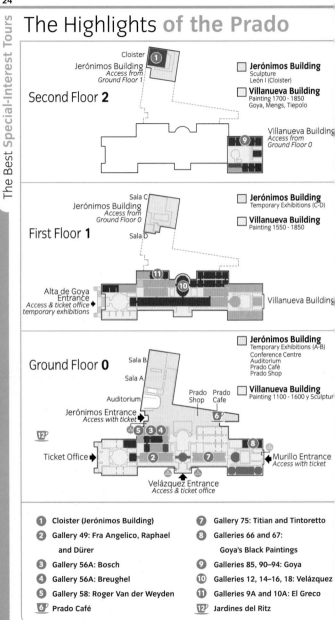

Jerónimos Building
Access from Ground Floor 1

Cloister ➊

☐ **Jerónimos Building**
Sculpture
León I (Cloister)

☐ **Villanueva Building**
Painting 1700 - 1850
Goya, Mengs, Tiepolo

Second Floor **2**

Villanueva Building
Access from Ground Floor 0

➒

Sala C
Jerónimos Building
Access from Ground Floor 0

Sala D

☐ **Jerónimos Building**
Temporary Exhibitions (C-D)

☐ **Villanueva Building**
Painting 1550 - 1850

First Floor **1**

➓ ⓫

Alta de Goya Entrance
Access & ticket office temporary exhibitions ➤

Villanueva Building

☐ **Jerónimos Building**
Temporary Exhibitions (A-B)
Conference Centre
Auditorium
Prado Café
Prado Shop

☐ **Villanueva Building**
Painting 1100 - 1600 y Sculpture

Ground Floor **0**

Sala B
Sala A

Auditorium

Jerónimos Entrance
Access with ticket ➤

Prado Shop   Prado Cafe

➏

➎ ➌ ➍ ➋ ➐ ➑

⓬

Ticket Office ➤

Murillo Entrance
Access with ticket ◄

Velázquez Entrance
Access & ticket office

➊ Cloister (Jerónimos Building)

➋ Gallery 49: Fra Angelico, Raphael and Dürer

➌ Gallery 56A: Bosch

➍ Gallery 56A: Breughel

➎ Gallery 58: Roger Van der Weyden

➏ Prado Café

➐ Gallery 75: Titian and Tintoretto

➑ Galleries 66 and 67:
   Goya's Black Paintings

➒ Galleries 85, 90–94: Goya

➓ Galleries 12, 14–16, 18: Velázquez

⓫ Galleries 9A and 10A: El Greco

⓬ Jardines del Ritz

The Prado is one of the world's greatest museums, with a rich collection originally gathered by the Habsburg monarchs. The Spanish art is unrivalled, and the extraordinary paintings of Velázquez and Goya are among the museum's finest treasures. The following tour includes my favorite galleries, but covers only a fraction of the entire collection. START: **Metro to Banco de España, then a five-minute walk.**

1 ★★ **Cloister (Jerónimos Building).** From the cavernous main entrance, follow the signs for the Claustro, a 16th-century cloister built for the nearby Jerónimos monastery and painstakingly moved, stone by stone, during the Prado's recent expansion. Now incorporated into the glassy new extension designed by Rafael Moneo (nicknamed Moneo's Cube), it's a graceful setting for several statues discovered in Hadrian's Villa. ⏱ *30 min.*

2 ★★★ **Gallery 49: Fra Angelico, Raphael, and Dürer.** Back in the main Villanueva Building, head for Gallery 49 and look for Fra Angelico's moving *Annunciation* (1426–7), in which the Angel announces Mary's impending conception in a haze of golden light. Raphael's *Portrait of a Cardinal* (c.1510) stands out for its masterful realism, from the perfect folds of the crimson silk to the calculation in the cold eyes. Around the same time, Dürer was painting the luscious diptych of *Adam* and *Eve* (1507), foregoing any extraneous background detail to focus attention on his sensuous nudes. ⏱ *1 hr.*

3 ★★★ **Gallery 56A: Bosch.** In Gallery 56A visitors pack themselves around the bizarre, surrealistic visions of the Flemish painter, Hieronymus Bosch. Thanks to Felipe II, the Prado contains several of his works. The unsettling *The Garden of Earthly Delights* is probably his most famous painting, equally beautiful and repellant. Divided into three panels, with Paradise on the left, Hell on the right, and the sins of the flesh in the center, it has defied interpretation since it was brought to court in the 16th century. ⏱ *30 min.*

4 ★★★ **Gallery 56A: Breughel.** I love Pieter Breughel's vibrant, earthy depictions of ordinary people, but his gloomier *The Triumph of Death* (1562) shows a desolate landscape in which dogs pick over the bones of the slaughtered. It is clearly influenced by Bosch, whom Breughel greatly admired, and it gives me the shivers. ⏱ *15 min.*

5 ★★★ **Gallery 58: Roger Van der Weyden.** Dominating one end of this small gallery is Roger Van der Weyden's electrifying *The Descent from the Cross* (c.1435). One of Van

Detail from Breughel's Triumph of Death (1562).

The Prado: Practical Matters

The entrance to the Prado is at the back through Rafael Moneo's glassy 2007 extension. Tickets, however, must be purchased (or Paseo del Arte tickets exchanged) at the Goya gate ticket offices found at the museum's northern end, prior to queuing up for entry. Note that post-renovation, most artworks described are likely to remain where they are, but floor plans are constantly being updated (pick up the latest at the information desk).

Paseo del Prado s/n: ☎ 91-330-28-00 or ☎ 902-10-70-77; www. museodelprado.es. Admission 6€ adults, 3€ students, under-18s free, when bought directly at ticket office; available in advance for 9€ adults, under-6s free; also part of Paseo del Arte ticket, 14.40€ (see box p 9). Mon–Sat 9am–8pm, Dec 24, Dec 31, Jan 6 9am–2pm. Closed: Mon, Dec 25, Jan 1, Good Friday, May 1. Audioguide available for permanent collection 3.50€, temporary exhibitions 3.50€, or both 5€. Metro: Banco de España.

der Weyden's largest works, it doesn't merely depict the moment when Christ's body is brought from the cross, but captures the cataclysmic pain of a mother who has lost her son. ⏱ 15 min.

🍴 **6 Prado Café.** Take a break at the modern café, near the main entrance. The self-service section is at the back, hidden behind the screens. Despite the sleek monochromatic décor, it is a bit like an airport café. Still, it's the only option within the museum. *Main entrance hall. $–$$.*

7 ★★★ Gallery 75: Titian and Tintoretto. The great Venetian painter Titian's portrait of *Charles V at the Battle of Mühlberg* (1548) is considered one of the finest equestrian portraits of all time. The psychological realism (just look at the king's weary expression despite his heroic pose) was a formal break with the purely classical style. Look out for Titian's equally masterful portrait

of *Felipe II With Armor* (1550–1), with the young king's hand uneasily resting on his helmet. This was the portrait sent to Mary Tudor of England during their marriage negotiations and, although it didn't please its subject, it clearly delighted his future wife. There are also works by another great Venetian colorist, Tintoretto, an ardent admirer of Titian (who was jealous, purportedly, of his young follower's talent), including the vivid early work *Christ Washing the Disciples' Feet* (1547), which manages to be both moving and intimate, despite its massive scale and some fine Tintoretto portraits, including the wry *Man with a Golden Chain* (1555). ⏱ 45 min.

8 ★★★ Galleries 66 and 67: Goya's Black Paintings. Enter the dim galleries that contain Goya's Black Paintings. In 1819, Goya—by now old, deaf, and sickened by war—moved to a small house outside Madrid, where he painted these bleak and sometimes horrifying murals directly onto the walls of his home. The most famous and graphic is *Saturn Devouring His Son*, which depicts a terrifying monster with dripping jaws, but I find *Semi-buried Dog*, utterly lost in a sickly yellow fog, unbearably sad. 🕐 *45 min.*

⑨ ★★★ Galleries 85, 90–94: Goya. Take the clumsy old lift up to the second floor for more Goya. A world away from the sinister Black Paintings, these galleries contain the cheerful designs made for a series of tapestries commissioned for the royal hunting lodge at El Prado. The pretty country scenes and frolicking children will banish any gloom. 🕐 *45 min.*

⑩ ★★★ Galleries 12, 14–16, 18: Velázquez. Gallery 12 is the centerpiece of the entire museum. Set against the pale brocade walls are the finest works by the great Spanish artist Velázquez, including *Las Meninas*, considered one of the greatest paintings of all time (see p 7: The Best in One Day). The monumental *Surrender of Breda* (1635) depicts a key moment in Spanish history: the handing over of the keys of the Flemish city of Breda to the Spanish general. In *The Jester Don Diego de Acedo*, Velázquez imbues his subject, one of more than a hundred dwarfs employed at the palace, with a dignity and humanity often denied them at court. By now, you are probably envying the red-cheeked revelers of *The Drinkers* (c. 1629) and longing for a drink yourself, but do explore the adjoining galleries to admire Velázquez's royal portraits. 🕐 *1 hr.*

⑪ ★★★ Galleries 9A and 10A: El Greco. Finally dip into Galleries 9a and 10a for a quick shot of the highly charged drama of El Greco. The Cretan-born artist trained in Venice and Rome before coming to Spain, where he remained for much of his life, but his art is utterly unlike any of his contemporaries. I like his late *Annunciation* (1596–1606), a swirling, ecstatic moment presided over by a dove emitting blinding light and a heavenly host. 🕐 *1 hr.*

⑫ ★★ Jardines del Ritz. You can't miss the Ritz, a white frothy Belle Époque-style palace that stands across the square from the Prado entrance. The terrace and gardens, through a white, wrought-iron entrance, is a refined and relaxing spot for a well-deserved post-Prado cocktail. *Plaza de la Lealtad.* ☎ *91-521-28-57. $–$$.*

Detail from the Surrender of Breda by Velazquez.

Highlights of the Paseo del Arte

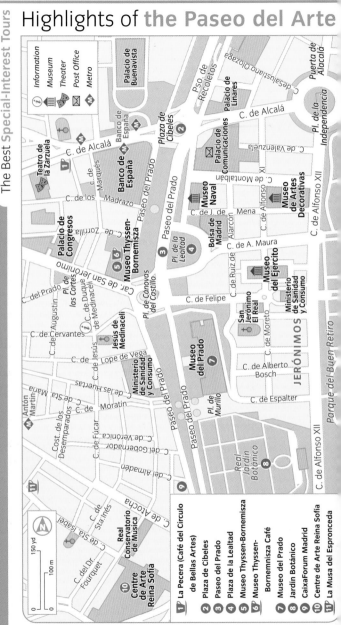

Legend:
- ⓘ Information
- 🏛 Museum
- 🎭 Theater
- ✉ Post Office
- ◈ Metro

1️⃣ La Pecera (Café del Círculo de Bellas Artes)
2️⃣ Plaza de Cibeles
3️⃣ Paseo del Prado
4️⃣ Plaza de la Lealtad
5️⃣ Museo Thyssen-Bornemisza
6️⃣ Museo Thyssen-Bornemisza Café
7️⃣ Museo del Prado
8️⃣ Jardín Botánico
9️⃣ CaixaForum Madrid
🔟 Centre de Arte Reina Sofía
1️⃣1️⃣ La Musa de Espronceda

The Paseo del Arte properly refers to Madrid's Big Three museums (the Prado, the Thyssen-Bornemisza, and the Reina Sofía), which are conveniently located within a few minutes' walk of each other. The highlights of the Prado are described on p 24, but below you'll find the best of the Thyssen and the Reina Sofía, along with the gardens and fountains found along the way. START: **Metro to Banco de España.**

1 ★★ **La Pecera (Café del Círculo de Bellas Artes).** Fortify yourself for a long day's sightseeing beneath the crystal chandeliers of this gorgeous Art Deco café. *Cl Alcalá 42.* ☎ *93-360-54-00. $–$$.*

2 ★ **Plaza de Cibeles.** The flamboyant statue of the goddess Cibeles in her chariot, surrounded by spurting fountains, has become the city's unofficial symbol. Behind Cibeles is an extravagant white palace, which is actually Madrid's main post office. I love the elaborate gilded letterboxes on the exterior, which add a dash of romance to the humdrum task of posting a letter. ⏰ *15 min. Metro: Banco de España.*

3 ★ **Paseo del Prado.** The Paseo del Prado is a relatively short boulevard that runs from the Plaza

de Cibeles to the Plaza del Emperador Carlos V in front of Atocha railway station, passing by some of the city's greatest art museums. In the center, a tree-shaded walkway is dotted with benches, fountains, and two children's playgrounds. Formerly called the Salón del Prado, where Madrileños would gather in their finery to flirt and gossip, the ornate carriages have now, unfortunately, given way to the roar of modern traffic. ⏰ *30 min. Metro: Banco de España or Atocha.*

4 ★ **Plaza de la Lealtad.** A semi-circular plaza, just off the Paseo del Prado on the left, contains a tall stone obelisk, set on a monumental plinth within a neat garden. This is the *Monument a Los Caidos por España* (Monument to the Fallen of Spain), first erected in the early 19th century in memory of the Madrileños

The tree-shaded walkway in the center of Paseo del Prado.

Special Activities in Madrid's Museums

Madrid's great museums all offer an excellent program of activities, which go beyond temporary exhibitions to include everything from family workshops and lectures to film screenings and concerts. Pick up programs at the start of your stay from the tourist office, or directly from museums. During the hot summer months, several offer late-night opening at least one day a week: these include the Museo Thyssen-Bornemisza, which opens its temporary exhibitions until 11pm Tues–Sat, and the Reina Sofía, which is open until 11pm on Saturday nights during August.

shot here by Napoleonic troops on May 2, 1808. In 1985 it was rededicated to all those who have died for Spain. An eternal flame burns perpetually on the monument's steps. ⏱ **10 min. Metro: Banco de España.**

⑤ ★★★ Museo Thyssen-Bornemisza. The late billionaire industrialist Baron Hans Heinrich Thyssen-Bornemisza devoted much of his life and wealth to the creation of one of the world's greatest private art collections. At the urging of his fifth wife, Carmen Cervera (crowned Miss Spain in 1961), he established the Thyssen-Bornemisza museum in Madrid in 1992, and allowed the

Spanish government to purchase most of it cheaply a year later. The museum neatly fills the gaps in the Prado, with a fine collection of so-called Italian primitives, early Flemish works, Renaissance and baroque painting, and an excellent array of Impressionists and post-Impressionists. I've selected the museum highlights below. Begin with the earliest works, on the second floor. My favorites here are Van der Weyden's exquisite *Madonna Enthroned* (c. 1433) in Room 3 and Jan van Eyck's superb diptych of *The Annunciation* (c. 1435–51, Room 3). In Room 5, Ghirlandaio's graceful Renaissance

Museo Thyssen-Bornemisza.

Museo del Prado.

Portrait of Giovanna Tornabuoni (1488) has become the museum's motif, Also note Hans Holbein's iconic *Portrait of King Henry VIII* (c.1534–1536). In Gallery 12, Caravaggio's drama-charged *Saint Catherine of Alexandria* (c.1597) heralds the baroque, his subject 'spotlighted' but surrounded by shadow. Head for Galleries 16–18 for wonderful Italian landscapes, including Canaletto's magical depictions of Venice. Rubens' fleshy *Venus and Cupid* (1606–12) is in Gallery 19. The collection continues on the first floor with some exquisite Dutch landscapes, interiors, and portraits in Galleries 22–26, including the sweeping skies of Jacob van Ruisdael's *View of Naarden* (1647). The final galleries of this floor are among the best, with a fabulous collection of Impressionist and post-Impressionist works (described in Best in One Day, see p 8), finishing up with harbingers of Cubism such as George Grosz's fiery, red *Metropolis* (1916–17) and August Macke's *Circus* (1913). The collection of modern art displayed in the Ground Floor galleries is a perfect introduction to the contemporary art at the Reina Sofía. Many of the great artists who were turning the art world upside-down in the early 20th century are represented in Galleries 41–44, from early Cubist works such

as Picasso's *Man with a Clarinet* (1911–12) to Mondrian's extraordinary *New York City, New York* (1940–42), stripped down to vertical lines and blocks of color. Galleries 45 and 46 contain Picasso's teasing *Harlequin with a Mirror* (1923), Miró's *Catalan Peasant with a Guitar* (1924), Rothko's *Green on Maroon* (1961), and Jackson Pollocks' *Brown and Silver I* (1951). ⏱ *2 hrs. Paseo del Prado 8.* ☎ *91-369-01-51. www. museothyssen.org. Admission to permanent collection 6€ adults, 4€ students, free for under-12s; temporary exhibition adm prices vary. Combined admission to permanent and temporary collection available. Also part of Paseo del Arte ticket, 14.40€. Tues–Sun 10am–7pm, ticket office closes 6.30pm. Closed Mon, Dec 25, Jan 1, May 1. Audioguide available to permanent and temporary collections. Metro: Banco de España.*

6️⃣ ★★ **Museo Thyssen-Bornemisza Café.** Tucked behind the rose garden at the main entrance to this museum is a delightful café with an expansive terrace and an airy modern interior. It's good for a coffee or the fixed-price lunch deal, but steer clear of over-priced sandwiches and salads. *Paseo del Prado.* ☎ *93-302-41-40. $–$$.*

CaixaForum's Vertical Garden.

7 ★★★ **Museo del Prado.** Continue walking down the Paseo del Prado and you'll see the grand old Prado itself on your left. It deserves a day to itself, so content yourself with a glance at the handsome columned exterior today. See Highlights of the Prado (p 24).

8 ★★ **Jardín Botánico.** The perfect antidote to art overload, this glorious 18th-century botanical garden is a verdant haven in the heart of the city. (see p 82). ⏱ *1 hr. Plaza*

Jardín Botánico.

de Murillo 1. ☎ *91-420-30-17. www. rjb.csic.es. Admission 2€ adults, 1€ students, free for under-10s. Metro Atocha.*

9 ★★ **CaixaForum Madrid.** Admire the striking, contemporary façade and the Vertical Garden as you stroll past the CaixaForum, one of the newest and most exciting art institutions. See Best in Two Days (see p 16).

10 ★★★ **Centre de Arte Reina Sofía.** The fabulous Reina Sofía museum houses an outstanding contemporary art collection. Newly expanded with a cutting-edge glass wing by Jean Nouvel, it is Madrid's most fashionable museum. The permanent collection is displayed on the second and fourth floors, accessed by a pair of swooping glass lifts with rooftop views. The biggest draw in the museum, and possibly the most famous artwork in the city (besides the Prado's *Las Meninas*), is Picasso's moving *Guernica* in Gallery 7 (see Best in One Day, p 9). The nearby galleries put *Guernica* into context, with other artworks created, like *Guernica*, for the Spanish Pavilion in Paris' International Exhibition of 1937, and a room devoted to Robert Capa's horrifying war photography

(Room 8B). But some of the greatest Spanish artists of the 20th century are also represented here: the highly personal abstraction of Joan Miró (Rooms 11 and 12); Salvador Dalí's nightmarish, Surrealist works (Room 9A); and the three-dimensional materialism of Antoni Tàpies (Room 12), perhaps Spain's most famous living artist. I particularly love Alberto Sanchéz ethereal, slim sculptures in Room 12C. Art from the late 1940s to the early 21st century is gathered on the fourth floor. As you leave the lift, look for Amparo Garrido's highly expressive large-scale photographs of dog's faces. My favorite works here are Henry Moore's sensuous, curvaceous sculptures in Room 17 and the electric blue paintings by French artist Yves Klein in Room 18. I also always enjoy the beautiful, light-infused views of Madrid by Antonio López García (Room 24) and the magnificent, large-scale creations by celebrated Basque sculptor, Eduardo Chillida (Rooms 34 and 35). There is a small selection of Minimal art by great American artists including Donald Judd and Ellsworth Kelly in Room 36, and the collection closes with four galleries dedicated to recent creations by Spanish and international artists. Don't miss Cristina Iglesias' enormous *Pavilion Suspended in a Room* (2005). *1 hr. Cl Santa Isabel 52.* ☎ *91-774-10-00. www.museoreinasofia.es. Admission to permanent collection 6€ adults, 3€ students, free for under-12s; temporary exhibition adm prices vary. Combined admission to permanent and temporary collection available. Also part of Paseo del Arte ticket, 14.40€. Mon, Wed–Sun 10am–9pm, ticket office closes 6.30pm. Closed Tues, Dec 24, Dec 25, Dec 31 Jan 1, Jan 6, May 1, May 15, Sept 7, Free Sat 2.30–9pm, Sun 10am–2.30pm, May 18, Oct 12, Dec 6. Audioguide available to permanent and temporary collections. Guided visits in Spanish only Mon and Wed 5pm, Sat 11pm. Metro: Atocha.*

🍵 ⓫ ★★ **La Musa del Espronceda.** A hip but relaxed hangout near the Reina Sofía, with a tapas bar serving Basque *pintxos* (slices of baguette with delectable toppings) plus a dining area. Blackboards are scrawled with the day's specials, and there's an exhibition space and screening room in the basement. *Cl Santa Isabel 17.* ☎ *91-539-12-84. $–$$.*

Museo Nacional Reina Sofia.

Royal Madrid

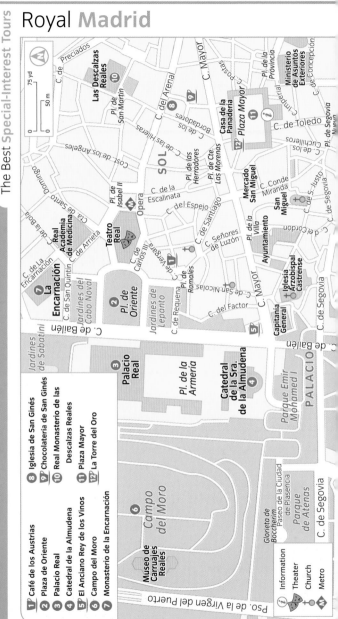

1 Café de los Austrias
2 Plaza de Oriente
3 Palacio Real
4 Catedral de la Almudena
5 El Anciano Rey de los Vinos
6 Campo del Moro
7 Monasterio de la Encarnación
8 Iglesia de San Ginés
9 Chocolatería de San Ginés
10 Real Monasterio de las Descalzas Reales
11 Plaza Mayor
12 La Torre del Oro

Information
Theater
Church
Metro

0   50 m
0   75 yd

Felipe II plucked Madrid from obscurity in 1561 to become Spain's permanent capital, but later monarchs really transformed the city from an overgrown village into a true European capital. From the splendid Plaza Mayor to the staggering baroque Royal Palace, this tour takes in the greatest Habsburg and Bourbon monuments. START: **Metro to Ópera.**

1 ★★ **Café de los Austrias.** One of my favorite cafés, this neighborhood classic has faded mirrors and worn marble columns. Glimpse the Royal Palace from the summer terrace. *Plaza de Ramales 1.* ☎ *91-559-84-36.* $.

2 ★ **Plaza de Oriente.** With its clipped gardens and fountains, gilded cafés, and views of the Opera House and the Royal Palace, this is a lavish square. ⏲ *20 min. Metro: Ópera. See p10, bullet* **8**.

3 ★★★ **Palacio Real.** In 1734, the old Royal Palace (built on the ruins of the Arabic fortress that once occupied this hill) was destroyed in a great fire. The new Bourbon monarchs decided that a vast baroque palace would remind the Spanish people and European monarchs of their power. Be thankful that Italian architect Juvarra's original plans were never carried out: his vision of a palace to vie with Versailles was over three times the size of the current mammoth edifice with its 3,000 rooms. Check the palace is open before you visit: although the current royal family resides at the modest palace of El Pardo, this is still used for special state functions and can close without warning. I recommend the audio guide over the guided tour. You'll get much the same information but can be more selective with your time. Among the rooms you really shouldn't miss are the extravagant **Throne Room**, with a fresco by the great Venetian painter Tiepolo; the **Gasparini Room**, used by Carlos III to receive guests and covered with elaborate baroque gold and silver; and the **Porcelain Room**, an eye-popping rococo vision encrusted

Explore the extravagant rooms in the Palacio Real.

What a Day for an Auto-de-Fé

The Spanish Inquisition was established by the 'Catholic Monarchs', Ferdinand and Isabella, in the late 15th century, but it reached the height of its power in the early 17th century. Felipe II, deeply religious and terrified of heresy, gave the Inquisition far-reaching powers to investigate any diversion from his rigid orthodoxy. Thousands were tried in the public ceremonies known as the auto-de-fé (which means 'act of faith') and those who failed to recant publicly were condemned to a terrible death. In just one day in 1680, more than 118 prisoners were tried, of whom 21 were burned alive.

with porcelain made in the royal factory that once stood in the Retiro gardens. Other highlights include the dazzling **Hall of Mirrors**, which took its inspiration from Versailles, the 19th-century **Gala Banqueting Hall**, and the musical instruments in the **Stradivarius Room**. The **Painting Gallery** contains some remarkable works by Velázquez, Caravaggio, and Goya. Off the vast Plaza de la Armería are two more museums: the **Royal Pharmacy** and the **Royal Armory**, which are part of the Royal Palace but visited with a separate admission ticket. I prefer to see the Royal

The neo-baroque Catedral de la Almudena.

Palace in small doses, and recommend leaving the latter two museums for another day (for descriptions, see Best in One Day, p 10, bullet ⑨. ⏲ 2½ hrs. Cl Bailén. ☎ 91-454-87-00. Admission to Palace, Pharmacy, and Royal Armory 10€ adults with guided visit, 6€ for students and children 5–16, or 8€ without guide, no concessions; guided visit to Palace, Pharmacy, Royal Armory, and Picture Gallery 11€ adults, 7€ for students and children 5–16; Picture Gallery only 2€, no concessions; Royal Armory only 3.40€ adults, 2.50€ students and children 5–16, free non-guided visits for EU-citizens Wed. Oct–Mar Mon–Sat 9.30am–5pm, Sun 9.30am–2pm; Apr–Sept Mon–Sat 9am–6pm, Sun 9am–3pm. Closed Jan 1, Jan 7, May 1, Sept 9, Oct 12, Dec 24, Dec 25, Dec 31. Metro: Ópera See p 10, bullet ⑨.*

④ ★★ **Catedral de la Almudena.** Outside the Royal Palace, the great dome of the Catedral de la Almudena is directly in front of you. Curiously, Madrid had no cathedral until 1993 when this rather dull, neo-baroque construction was finally completed. It remains Spain's most important cathedral, where royal births, christenings, and weddings are celebrated (including Prince Felipe's marriage to Leticia, a

glamorous TV journalist, in 2004).
🕐 *5 min. Free. Daily 10am–7.30pm, no entry to tourists during mass. Metro: Ópera. See p 10, bullet ⑩.*

5̄ ★ El Anciano Rey de los Vinos. The century-old El Anciano Rey de los Vinos offers wines, including traditional *vermú* (a fortified wine) from the barrel, to go with the old-fashioned tapas. Perfect for parched and footsore palace visitors. *Cl Bailén 19.* ☎ *91-559-53-32. $–$$.*

6̄ ★★ kids Campo del Moro. Behind the northern façade of the Royal Palace, just beyond the Plaza de Oriente, are the elegant Sabatini Gardens, a calm oasis after the rich palace interiors. Beyond them, you can take the Cuesta de San Vicente downhill towards the entrance to the Casa del Campo, the former Royal Gardens that spread down the hill behind the Royal Palace. In the late 19th century, these shaded pathways, flower gardens, pools, and fountains were laid out in the Romantic English style. Quiet, cool, and beautiful, this is one of the loveliest spots, with spectacular views of the Royal Palace, elegantly framed by sweeping avenues. 🕐 *45 min. Entrances on Paseo Virgen del Puerto and Cuesta de san Vicente.* ☎ *91-454-88-00. Free admission. Open Oct–Mar Mon-Sat 10–6, Sun 9–6.*

7̄ ★★ kids Monasterio de la Encarnación. Once you've scrambled back up the hill from the Campo de Moro, make for the Monasterio de la Encarnación, established for royal nuns. For a description, see Best in Two Days, p 14). 🕐 *1 hr. Plaza de la Encarnación 1.* ☎ *91-454-88-00. www.patrimonio nacional.es. Admission 3.60€ adults, 2.90€ students and children 5–16, free Wed to EU-citizens; combined admission ticket with Monasterio de Las Descalzas Reales 6€ adults, 5–16 4.90€ students and children. June–Sept Tues–Sat 10am–8pm, Sun 10am–3pm; Oct–May Tues, Wed, Thurs, Sat 10.30am–12.45pm,*

Monasterio de la Encarnación.

Iglesia de San Ginés.

4–5.45pm. Fri 10.30am–12.45pm, Sun and public hols 11am–1.45pm. Closed Jan 1, Easter weekend, May 1, May 15, Sept 9, Dec 24, Dec 25, Dec 31. Metro: Ópera.

⑧ ★ Iglesia de San Ginés. This pretty church is set back from the Calle Arenal. Although the current version dates mostly from the 17th century, the original church was founded in the 13th century and is one of Madrid's oldest. In the adjoining Capilla de Sant Cristo, you can just make out the statue of Christ amid the gloom—it's one of the most venerated statues in the city. 🕙 *15 min.*

⑨ ★ kids Chocolatería de San Ginés. Join locals taking a break from shopping, and dunk the scrumptious *churros* (long, fried dough sticks) into the gloopy hot chocolate for the ultimate afternoon pick-me-up. *Cl Montsió 3.* ☎ *93-302-41-40. $–$$.*

⑩ ★★ Real Monasterio de las Descalzas Reales. This is the finest surviving royal convent, established by Juana of Austria, widowed at just 19. The original building was erected over the palace in which she was born, and is still home to a small closed community of nuns (you might glimpse them at work in the pretty garden). Thanks to its royal connections, the convent became one of the richest religious institutions in the kingdom, although most of its treasures were subsequently sold during hard times. Some have survived and are described on the (mandatory) guided tour. These tours are officially in Spanish only, but many of the guides are multilingual. The lavish 16th-century staircase, with its

Real Monasterio de las Descalzas Reales.

Plaza Mayor.

wonderful trompe l'oeil frescoes (look out for Felipe IV with his family), provides a plush entrance to the convent—and a reminder of the powerful connections enjoyed by the blue-blooded nuns. The lovely cloister, with its peeling frescoes, is the most romantic part of the convent, and I always wish the guide would allow more time to explore the tiny side chapels. Most of the convent's scant paintings are copies of important works or by minor artists, but there are one or two great pieces among them, including a portrait by Zurbarán and a beatific virgin by Luís Morales. The convent is proudest of its fine tapestry collection, designed by Rubens and woven in Brussels. A mirror—supposedly the only one in the convent—allows visitors to see the sketch on the back of the tapestry. There's also a recreation of a spartan cell, complete with scourge to mortify the flesh. See p14.

🕐 *1 hr. Plaza de las Descalzas s/n.* ☎ *91-454-88-00. www.patrimonio nacional.es. Admission 5€ adults, 4€ students, children 5–16, free Wed to EU-citizens; combined admission ticket with Real Monasterio de la Encarnación 6€ adults, students and children 5–16 4.90€. June–Sept Tues–Sat 10am–8pm, Sun 10am–3pm; Oct–May Tues, Wed, Thurs, Sat* 10.30am–12.45pm and 4–5.45pm. Fri 10.30am–12.45pm, Sun and public hols 11am–1.45pm. Closed Jan 1, Easter weekend, May 1, May 15, Sept 9, Dec 24, Dec 25, Dec 31. Metro: Sol. Metro: Sol. Metro: Hospital de San Pau or Sagrada Familia (and a 10-minute walk along Av. de Gaudi).*

⓫ ★★★ **Plaza Mayor.** Completed in 1620, the Plaza Mayor was the magnificent showpiece of the new Habsburg capital. The square could accommodate about a third of the city's total population and became a splendid theater for royal pronouncements, public executions, lavish festivals, and bullfights. The Inquisition's ghastly torture chambers and dungeons were located beneath the square, and the mass trials of heretics, called *autos de fé*, were among the most theatrical and terrifying of all the spectacles enacted here (see box, p 36). See also p 7. 🕐 *45 min. Metro: Sol.*

⓬ ★ **La Torre del Oro.** Underneath the Arco de Triunfo, this cheerful Andalusian tavern is filled with bull's heads and photographs of famous *corridas*. Tuck into tapas, and see if you can spot the *toreros* among the tourists at the bar. *Plaza Mayor 20.* ☎ *91-366-50-16. $–$$.*

The Best Special-Interest Tours

Downtown Madrid: the Gran Vía

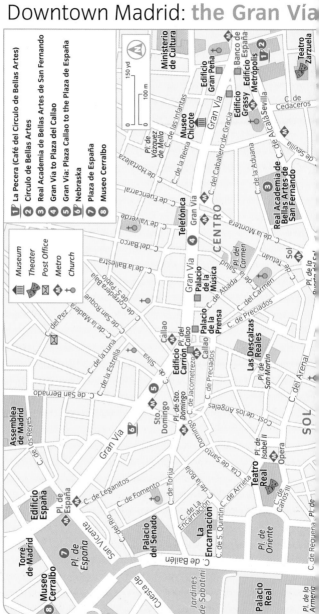

Museum	
Theater	
Post Office	
Metro	
Church	

The Gran Vía was built through the medieval heart of the city in the early 20th century. Splashed with neon and spiked with thrusting skyscrapers, it showed the world that Madrid was as bold and forward-thinking as New York, Chicago, or any other great metropolis. It has undoubtedly lost much of its pizzazz in the last century, but just gaze upwards to recapture the jazz-age optimism. START: **Metro to Banco de España.**

1 ★★ **La Pecera (Café del Círculo de Bellas Artes).** One of the loveliest Art Deco buildings in the city, now a dynamic art institution (see below), this contains a fabulously over-the-top café for coffee or breakfast. *Cl Alcalá 42.* ☎ *93-360-54-00. $–$$.*

2 ★★ **Círculo de Bellas Artes.** Curiously, the same architect behind the huge wedding-cake post office on the Plaza de Cibeles created this luscious Art Deco gem, with its billowing curves and enormous picture windows. Originally built as a private club, it's now home to one of the city's best art institutions. Besides the fabulous café-bar, there is a cinema, exhibition spaces, a lecture hall, and resplendent ballroom. ⏱ *20 min. Cl Alcalá 4.* ☎ *91-360-54-00.*

3 ★★ **Real Academia de Bellas Artes de San Fernando.** Emerging from the Círculo de Bellas Artes, look down Calle Alcalá to your left to see one of its most historic art institutions: the Real Academia de Bellas Artes, established in 1773 and housed in a restrained Baroque palace. Its magnificent art collection is overshadowed by the Prado but is considered one of the finest in Spain. Here, you'll find works by Zurbarán, Morales, Goya, Rubens, Caravaggio, and Picasso. ⏱ *1 hr. Cl Alcalá 13.* ☎ *91-523-15-99. http://rabasf.insde.es. Admission 3€ adults, 1.50€ students and seniors, free for under-18s; free on Wed, May 18, Oct 12, and Dec 6. Tues–Fri 9am–2pm, 4–7pm, Sat 9am–2.30pm, 4–7pm, Sun–Mon and public hols 9am–2.30pm. Closed Mon, Dec 25–26 and Jan 1–6. Metro: Sevilla.*

4 ★★ **Gran Vía to Plaza del Callao.** The Gran Vía begins where

Art Deco interior of Círculo de Bellas Artes.

'Howitzer Alley'

When Civil War broke out in Spain in 1936, the Republican government, certain that Madrid would fall, fled to safety in Valencia. But, against all odds, the city held out, and the famous battle cry of its brave citizens, 'No Pasarán' (They shall not pass), was an inspiration for the entire country. In 1939, as the war came to its bitter end, Madrid was finally forced to capitulate—the last city in Spain to fall to the Nationalists. During the war years, the Madrileños were under constant attack, and the Gran Vía was nicknamed the Avenida de los Obuses ('Howitzer Alley') or the Avenida del Quince y Medio ('Fifteen and a Half Avenue'), referring to the huge shells that continually rained down. Even now, pockmarks are visible on the Telefónica building, which, as the highest building in the city, came under constant bombardment.

it merges with the Calle Alcalá. This junction is one of the most-photographed for its fine ensemble of flamboyant, turn-of-the-20th-century constructions. On the left, the **Edificio Metropolis** (Calle Alcalá, No. 37) is a lavish eclectic building topped with a winged angel; at Gran Vía 1, the fanciful **Grassy** building is topped with a neo-Renaissance cupola; opposite, at Gran Vía 2, is the curvaceous **Edificio Gran Peña**, still home to the city's most exclusive gentleman's club. Beyond them, farther up Gran Vía at No. 28, gleams the vast white **Telefónica** building, the first skyscraper in the city, built by an American architect on the Chicago model in the 1920s. Strolling up the Gran Vía, look out for the Art Deco **Chicote** cocktail bar on the right at No. 12. Its walls are still

The Edificio Metropolis, Gran Vía.

Don Quijote and Sancho Panza, Plaza de España.

adorned with photos of the rich and famous from Frank Sinatra to Ava Gardner, who once gathered at this infamous celebrity haunt. ⏱ *45 min. Metro: Banco de España or Callao.*

5 ★★ **Gran Vía: Plaza Callao to the Plaza de España.** The attractive Art Deco buildings clustered around the Plaza Callao are among my favorites in the whole city. Inspired by the innovative and daring new constructions mushrooming in North American cities, many were built as cinemas and still are, some advertising the films with huge, hand-painted billboards. Look out for the gorgeous streamlined curves of the **Edificio Carrión** (Gran Vía 41), which houses the Capitol theater; the ambitious **Palacio de la Prensa** (Plaza del Callao 4, usually adorned with immense hand-painted cinema posters); and the dainty **Palacio de la Música** (Gran Vía 35). The third stretch of the Gran Vía, up to the Plaza España, was mostly built after the Civil War and the mediocrity of the architecture reflects the repressive regime of the time. This stretch is, however, packed with all the best Spanish chain stores, from Zara to Mango, offering plenty of great shopping. ⏱ *30 min. Metro: Callao.*

6 **Nebraska.** One of a small chain of homegrown fast-food cafés, this brightly lit (and, unusually for Spain, smoke-free) spot is very popular with locals. Stop for an ice cream or a coffee, but don't bother with lunch—you'll get a better deal elsewhere. *Gran Vía 55.* ☎ *91-547-16-35. $–$$.*

7 ★ **Plaza de España.** The Plaza de España is a legacy of the Franco era, and none the better for it. It is overlooked by dreary office blocks and two dull 1950s skyscrapers, the Edificio España and the Torre de Madrid. The parched and dusty square is redeemed by the fountain, which includes a bronze statue of Cervantes' great creation Don Quijote, with sidekick Sancho Panza. For a clichéd but fun tourist photo, there's nowhere better. ⏱ *10 min.*

8 ★★★ **Museo Cerralbo.** Tucked behind the Plaza de España is the spellbinding Cerralbo museum, a wonderfully eclectic and intimate collection of artworks gathered in a charming 19th-century mansion. Unfortunately, the museum has been closed for several years for refurbishment, and, although it is slated to re-open in 2009, this date remains uncertain. ⏱ *(if open) 1 hr. Metro: Plaza de España.*

Madrid's Quirky Museums

- *i* — Information
- 🚉 — Rail Station
- ◆ — Metro

1. Real Fábrica de Tapices
2. Museo Taurino
3. Los Timbales
4. Museo Sorolla
5. Museo Lázaro Galdiano
6. Confitería Rialto
7. Museo de América
8. Museo del Traje
9. Bokado

Madrid's trio of outstanding art museums steals the lime-light, but there are plenty of curious collections scattered around the city, from the extraordinary treasures of South American civilizations to Spanish fashions from the last millennia. This tour includes metro instructions to help you get around. START: **Metro to Atocha.**

1 ★★ Real Fábrica de Tapices. I love this museum for the thrill of history it offers. The lavish tapestries are still made on enormous wooden looms just as they were in the early 18th century, when Felipe V founded the factory. Goya's first job in Madrid was creating the elaborate tapestries used to decorate the Royal Palaces. Once there were hundreds of workers; now there are just a handful, but their painstaking labor, threading the bright skeins of wool through the loom, is riveting. Hop back on the metro, change at Sol, and emerge at Ventas. ⏱ *1 hr. Cl Fuentarrabia 2.* ☎ *91-434-05-50. Admission 3.50€ adults, free for under-12s. Mon–Fri 10am–2pm. Metro: Menéndez Pelayo Espanya.*

2 Museo Taurino. I am firmly against bullfighting, but it is part of

The former home of Valencian painter Joaquin Sorolla.

Spain's cultural fabric, and the impressive Ventas bullring is considered its 'cathedral' in Spain. The adjoining museum contains the elaborate costumes of famous *toreros* such as Manolete, who was gored here in 1947, along with the heads of the feistiest bulls. To reach the next stop, take the metro three stops to Rubén Dario. ⏱ *30 min. Cl Alcalá 237.* ☎ *91-725-18-57. Free admission. Mon–Fri 9.30am–2.30pm. Metro: Ventas.*

3 ★★ Los Timbales. Going strong since 1929, this local classic is decorated with colorful tiles, bulls' heads, and photographs of famous matadors. Drop in for tapas or a dish of steaming *rabo de toro* (braised bull's tail). *Cl Alcalá 227.* ☎ *91-725-07-68. $–$$.*

4 ★★ Museo Sorolla. The charming 19th-century home of the Valencian painter Joaquín Sorolla (1853–1923) is set in a small but enchanting garden. Fountains trickle into tiled pools, birds twitter among the greenery, and the little bower is ideal for enjoying a picnic. Inside the house, some of Sorolla's finest Impressionist-style works have been gathered in elegant galleries, and his studio is just as he left it. It's a five-minute walk to the next stop. ⏱ *1 hr. Paseo General Martínez Campos 37.* ☎ *91-310-15-84. http://museosorolla.mcu.es Admission 3.50€ adults, free under-18s and over-65s. Free Sun, May 18, Oct 12, Dec 6. Tues–Sat 9.30am–8pm, Sun and public hols 10am–3pm,*

Museo Lázaro Galdiano.

open until 11.30pm Wed and Thurs from mid-June till late-Sept. Metro Rubén Darío, Gregorio Marañón.

5 ★★ **Museo Lázaro Galdiano.** See The Best in Three Days, p20. To reach the next stop, take the metro from Nuñez de Balboa to Moncloa, changing at Callao. 🕐 1 hr. Metro: Nuñez de Balboa.

6 ★★ **Confitería Rialto.** Lines always form outside this great pastry shop near the Nuñéz Balboa metro stop. It's famous for the delectable *moscovitas*—a divine combination of chocolate, wafer,

The Museo de América houses treasures from the Inca, Mayan and Aztec cultures.

cream, and almonds. Order a couple of bags—you won't want to share. Cl Nuñez de Balboa 86. ☎ 91-426-37-77. $–$$.

7 ★ **Museo de América.** This large, old-fashioned museum contains treasures from the great Mayan, Inca, and Aztec cultures of the Americas. Few tourists make it here, but there are some interesting artifacts, typically brought back to Spain by rapacious early explorers of the New World. There are terrifying masks, used in war, fine jewelry, painted manuscripts, and mysterious carved stones. Take the steep steps opposite the museum entrance down to the main road, turn right, and you'll soon see the Museo del Traje next to the roundabout. 🕐 45 min. Av Reyes Católicos 6. ☎ 91-549-26-41. http://museodeamerica.mcu.es. Admission 3.01€ adults, free to under-18s and over-65s. Free Sun, May 18, Oct 12, Dec 6. Metro: Moncloa.

8 ★★ kids **Museo del Traje.** Madrid's costume museum opened in 2004, and has become—fittingly—quite fashionable. The permanent collection (which rotates regularly) contains everything from the heartbreakingly tiny medieval burial gown of the Infanta María to the jaunty costumes of the Madrileño *majos* and

Real Madrid

Real Madrid is one of the richest, most successful, and most famous football teams in the world. Founded in 1902, the club has won La Liga 31 times, the Copa del Rey 17 times, and the European Cup a record nine times. Tickets for matches at the home stadium, the Santiago Bernabéu (which has its own metro stop), are much sought after—particularly when Los Merengues ('the meringues', nicknamed for their white strip) play archrivals FC Barcelona. Fans of all ages will enjoy the Real Madrid museum that charts the club's history and includes a tour of the stadium. Estadio Santiago Bernabéu (tickets from Window 10, near Gate 7, on the Paseo de la Castellana), ☎ 91-398-43-70 or 902-30-17-09. www.realmadrid.es. Admission adults 15€, under-14s 10€. Mon–Sat 10.30am–7.30pm, Sun and public hols 10.30am–6.30pm. Limited access on match days.

majas (working class dandies) depicted by Goya. Fashionistas will love the delicate designer pieces from the 20th century, ranging from embroidered flapper dresses to chic eveningwear by the legendary Balenciaga. Fashion-conscious teenagers will love this place, but children of all ages will enjoy trying on the old-fashioned outfits, as well as strutting down the catwalk at the exit. There's a great café to relax in after your visit. ⏱ *45 min. Av. Juan de Herrera 2.* ☎ *91-550-47-00. Admission 3€*

adults, 1.50€ students, free for under-18s and over-65s. Tues–Sat 9.30am–7pm, Sun and public hols 10am–3pm, open until 10.30pm on Thurs in July and Aug.

🍴 ★★ **Bokado.** This chic restaurant (see Dining, p100) in the Museo del Traje has an adjoining café, with a pleasant summer terrace overlooking the fountains and velvety lawns. On a hot summer evening, it's blissful. *Cl Elisabets 9.* ☎ *93-270-13-63. $.*

Museo del Traje.

Madrid **for** Kids

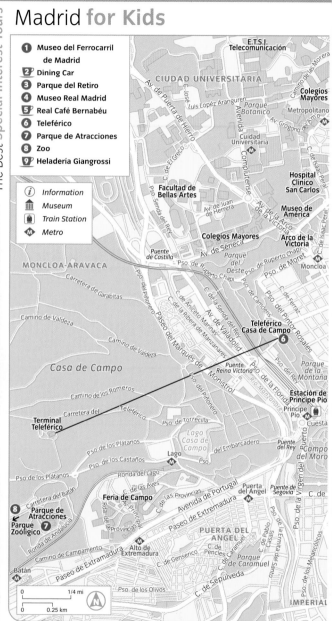

1. Museo del Ferrocarril de Madrid
2. Dining Car
3. Parque del Retiro
4. Museo Real Madrid
5. Real Café Bernabéu
6. Teleférico
7. Parque de Atracciones
8. Zoo
9. Heladeria Giangrossi

- (i) Information
- Museum
- Train Station
- Metro

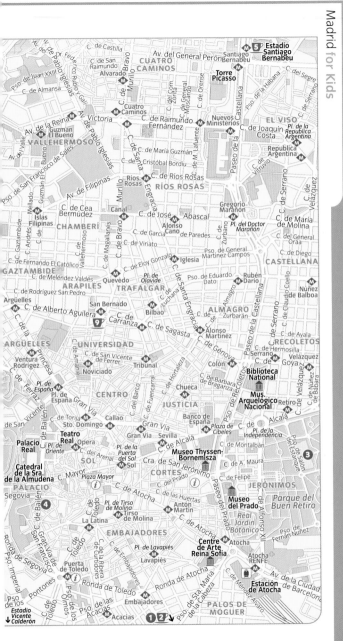

Madrid's art museums may leave your children cold, but the city has plenty to offer younger visitors. They can mess about on boats, ride a steam train, float across the city in a cable car, roar at the lions in the zoo, or just kick a ball around one of the glorious parks. Children are indulged in all but the haughtiest restaurants, and my son has friends in every tapas bar in the city. START: **Metro to Delicias.**

1 ★★ **Museo del Ferrocarril de Madrid.** Justifiably a big favorite with Madrileño families, the hugely enjoyable train museum has a collection of historic trains to clamber over and pretend to drive, plus model railways and a beautifully restored 1920s dining car. It's free on Saturdays, which means crowds, but your children may enjoy running around with the Spanish youngsters. ⏱ *1 hr. Paseo de las Delicias 61.* ☎ *902-22-88-22. www. museodelferrocarril.org. Admission adults 4€, children 4–12 2.50€, free for under-4s; free on Sat. Tues–Sun 10am–3pm, closed Aug. Metro: Delicias.*

2 ★ **Dining Car.** I love this beautifully restored dining car, with its plush wooden paneling, flip-up leather seats, and pretty table lamps. *Museo del Ferrocarril.* ☎ *902-22-88-22. $.*

3 ★★ **Boating in the Parque del Retiro.** The glorious Retiro Gardens are heaven for kids of all ages. There are several play areas (including an adventure playground) clustered near the Puerta de Alcalá entrance, but best of all is the magnificent boating lake. Bring a bag of breadcrumbs to feed the fat carp or take out one of the rowing boats for a gentle jaunt. If you'd rather let someone (or something) else do the work, take a trip on a small solar-powered boat. ⏱ *1 hr. No phone. Parque del Retiro. Rowing boats, available 10am–dusk, 4.40€; solar-powered boat trip 1.15€ adults, free for under-2s. 10am–dusk. Metro: Retiro or Banco de España.*

4 ★★ **Museo Real Madrid.** See box, p 47 (Madrid's Quirky Museums). ⏱ *1 hr.*

Kids' Attractions around Madrid

There are plenty of big theme parks around Madrid to keep children happy for at least a day. Hang out with Daffy Duck and Yogi Bear at the Parque Warner (www.parquewarner.com); enjoy the penguins and flamingoes at the botanic park, Faunia (www.faunia.es); or beat the summer heat at the Aquopolis water park (www.aquopolis.es). Children can even learn to ski at Spain's only indoor ski-centre Xanadú (www.millsxanadu.com), open year-round.

8 ★ **Zoo.** A short walk beyond the Parque de Atracciones is Madrid's Zoo-Aquarium. Pandas, elephants, tigers, dolphins, and sea lions will keep your children very happily entertained. The very young will love La Pequeña Granja (the little zoo), with lambs and donkeys for them to pet. ⏱ *2 hrs. Casa de Campo.* ☎ *91-512-37-70. Admission adults 17.90€, children 3–7 and seniors 14.50€, free for under-3s. Opening hours vary: check the website. Closed Jan. Metro: Casa de Campo, or cable car and 15-minute walk.*

9 ★ **Heladeria Giangrossi.** Once back in the city center, treat your kids (and yourself) to a sumptuous Italian ice cream prepared with the freshest ingredients and no additives. I'm addicted to their famous *Dulce de Leche* (caramel) ice cream. *Cava Baja, 40.* ☎ *902-44-41-30. $.*

Thrills in the Parque de Atracciones.

Boating lake in Parque del Retiro.

5 ★ **Real Café Bernabéu.** A sleekly designed restaurant and café with incomparable views of one of the world's most famous football stadiums. *Av Concha Espina, 1 (in stadium, Gate 30).* ☎ *91-458-36-67. $–$$.*

6 ★★ **Teleférico.** See the Best in Three Days, p 21, for all about this cable car. ⏱ *30 min. Paseo del Pintor Rosales s/n.* ☎ *91-541-11-18. www.teleferico.com. Metro: Argüelles.*

7 ★ **Parque de Atracciones.** For thrill-seekers of all ages, there's nowhere better than Madrid's Attraction Park in the Casa del Campo. Older kids will love the Tornado rollercoaster or the head-spinning Rotor, while smaller children can enjoy a host of gentler rides. ⏱ *2 hrs. Casa de Campo.* ☎ *91-563-29-00. www.parquede atracciones.es. Admission and unlimited rides 27.50€ adults, children 3–6 and seniors 18€, free for under-3s. Opening hours vary: check the website. Metro: Casa de Campo, or cable car and a 15-minute walk.*

Tapas tour **in Madrid**

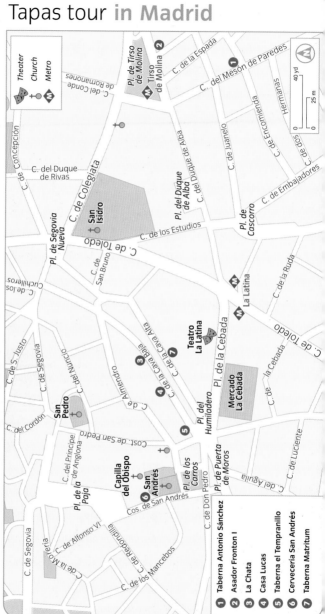

1. Taberna Antonio Sánchez
2. Asador Fronton I
3. La Chata
4. Casa Lucas
5. Taberna el Tempranillo
6. Cervecería San Andrés
7. Taberna Matritum

Tapas is central to Madrid's culinary scene, and a tour of the city's tapas bars is one of the most convivial and enjoyable gourmet experiences anywhere. I've chosen one of the most popular bar districts in the city, La Latina, and so try to visit during the week to avoid the crowds. START: **Metro to Plaça de Catalunya.**

The colorful façade of La Chata.

1 ★★★ **Taberna Antonio Sánchez.** This old-fashioned tavern was founded by an ex-torero, and is decorated with bull's heads, photographs, and newspaper articles. Pull up a wooden bench and order the *chipirones en su tinta* (baby squid), the classic Madrileño *callos* (tripe), or the homemade *croquetas.* ⏱ *30 min. Cl Mesón de*

Taberna Antonio Sánchez.

Paredes 13. ☎ *91-539-78-26. Metro: Tirso de Molina.*

2 ★★ **Asador Fronton I.** This rustic Navarrese restaurant is famous for its roast meats, but also serves delectable tapas, including *pimientos de piquillo* (stuffed peppers), out on the huge and popular terrace on the Plaza Tirso de Molina. ⏱ *30 min. Plaza Tirso de Molina 7.* ☎ *91-369-16-17. Metro: Tirso de Molina.*

3 ★★ **La Chata.** Cava Baja descends from the Plaza Segovia, jam-packed with some of the finest tapas bars. La Chata is a *castizo* (genuine) tavern, with atmosphere and bullfighting memorabilia. The house specialty is the *rabo de toro* (stewed bull's tail), but I prefer the Andaluz-style fried fish *(fritura de pescado)* with a glass of wine. ⏱ *30 min. Cl Cava Baja 24.* ☎ *91-366-14-58. Closed Tues and Wed lunchtimes. Metro: Alonso Martínez.*

4 ★★★ **Casa Lucas.** Farther down on the right, tiny Casa Lucas has an excellent selection of wines

Tapas for Beginners

Tapas in Madrid range from simple dishes of olives to gourmet creations prepared with champagne and foie gras. But most traditional bars in the city serve the following classics. *Croquetas*, mashed potato croquettes, come with different fillings, usually *jamón* (ham) or *bacalao* (cod). *Patatas bravas*, chunks of fried potato smothered in a spicy sauce, are said to have been invented here. *Tortilla*, thick potato omelet, is another classic. Many places serve shellfish, conserved in oil and vinegar: try *mejillones* (mussels), *almejas* (clams), or *anchoas* (anchovies). Grilled prawns (*gambas*), sometimes served in a garlic sauce (*al ajillo*) are popular too. These are all commonly accompanied with a glass of draught beer (*una caña*) or wine (*vino tinto* is red, *blanco* is white, *rosado* is rosé). As well as hams and cheeses, a wide range of charcuterie is commonly available, including *morcilla* (black pudding or blood sausage). For the adventurous, the classic Madrileño favorite is *callos* (tripe).

by the glass and the tapas are fresh and creative. ⏱ *30 min. Cl Cava Baja 30.* ☎ *91-365-08-04. Closed Wed lunchtime. Metro: La Latina.*

⑤ ★★★ Taberna el Tempranillo. A stroll down Cava Baja, there are more great wines to sample here and another range of tapas. The hams, which include a selection of unusual cuts, are always a tempting option. ⏱ *30 min. Cl Cava Baja 30.* ☎ *91-364-15-32. Metro: La Latina.*

Taberna Matritum.

⑥ ★★★ Cervecería San Andrés. Cava Baja emerges into the Plaza del Humilladero and almost opposite is the Cervecería San Andrés, with a large summer terrace. The tapas are basic but flavorsome, with classics such as *patatas bravas* to soak up the alcohol. ⏱ *30 min. Cl Cava Baja 30.* ☎ *91-364-15-32. Metro: La Latina.*

⑦ ★★★ Taberna Matritum. Parallel to Cava Baja is another bar-lined street, the Cava Alta. On the right is the Taberna Matritum, intimate and elegant, which also specializes in wines. They have an extensive list, which includes unusual boutique labels and rare vintages. Ask the helpful staff for advice. Among my favorite tapas are the eggplants (aubergines) baked with sun-dried tomatoes, and they also have delicious desserts. If you have the strength, you can continue up Cava Alta to find numerous excellent tapas bars, including Bibendum at No. 13, and Cava Blanca 7. ⏱ *30 min. Cl Cava Alta 16.* ☎ *91-365-82-37. Evenings only except at weekends. Metro: La Latina.* ●

Santa Ana: **Barrio de las Letras**

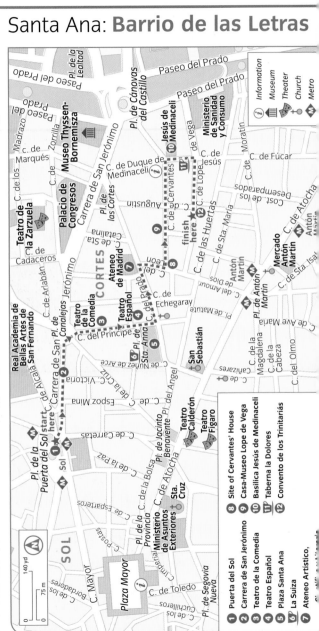

Information
Museum
Theater
Church
Metro

Paseo del Prado
Pl. de la Lealtad
Paseo del Prado
Paseo del Prado
Pl. de Cánovas del Castillo
C. de los
C. de
Marqués
Madrazo
C. de Zorrilla
Museo Thyssen-Bornemisza
Carrera de San Jerónimo
C. de Duque de Medinaceli
Pl. de las Cortes
Palacio de Congresos
Teatro de la Zarzuela
C. de Cadaceros
Carrera de San Jerónimo
CORTES
Pl. de Sta. Catalina
Agustín
Ateneo de Madrid
C. del Prado
Jesús de Medinaceli
C. de Jesús
Ministerio de Sanidad y Consumo
de Vega
C. de Moratín
C. de Fúcar
Cost. de los Desemparados
Mercado Antón Martín
C. de Atocha
Antón Martín
C. de Cervantes
C. de Lope
C. de las Huertas
C. de Sta. María
Pl. de Antón Martín
Antón Martín
C. de Sta. Isa
finish here
C. de León
C. del Amoun
de Dios
Pl. de Matute
San Sebastián
C. de la Magdalena
C. de la Cabeza
C. de Ave María
C. del Olmo
Real Academia de Bellas Artes de San Fernando
C. de Alcalá
C. de Ariabán
C. de Canalejas
Carrera de San Jerónimo
Teatro de la Comedia
Teatro Español
C. del Príncipe
Pl. de Sta. Anna
C. del Prado
C. de Echegaray
Pl. del Ángel
C. de Jacinto Benavente
C. de Núñez de Arce
C. de la Cruz
C. de la Victoria
Espoz Mina
Pl. de la Puerta del Sol
Sol
start here
C. de Carretas
C. de la Bolsa
C. de Atocha
Teatro Calderón
Teatro Fígaro
C. de las
San Jerónimo
Santa Cruz
Pl. de la Provincia
Ministerio de Asuntos Exteriores
C. Imperial
C. Cañizares
Plaza Mayor
C. Mayor
C. de los Bordadores
C. de Esparteros
C. de Postas
SOL
Pl. de Segovia Nueva
C. de Cuchilleros
C. de Segovia
C. de Toledo

140 yd
75 m
0

SOL

1 Puerta del Sol
2 Carrera de San Jerónimo
3 Teatro de la Comedia
4 Teatro Español
5 Plaza Santa Ana
6 La Suiza
7 Ateneo Artístico,

8 Site of Cervantes' House
9 Casa-Museo Lope de Vega
10 Basílica Jesús de Medinaceli
11 Taberna la Dolores
12 Convento de los Trinitarias

Santa Ana has long been the most bohemian barrio in Madrid. Writers and dramatists such as Cervantes and Lope de Vega lived (and bickered) here during the Golden Age of the 16th century, and intellectuals argued about poetry and politics in the legendary 19th-century cafés and bars. Now it's a fashionable nightlife district, and memories of literary giants live on in the historic streets. START: **Metro to Sol.**

1 ★ **Puerta del Sol.** See p 15, Best in Two Days, for all about this central square.

2 ★ **Carrera de San Jerónimo.** From the Puerta del Sol, walk down the C/a de San Jerónimo, pausing to stop at a plaque on the corner with Calle Victoria, which remembers a long-gone but legendary literary café, the **Fontana del Oro**. Farther on, you can admire the delectable pastries laid out in the windows of **Casa Mira**. Beyond it, at No. 8, is **L'Hardy**, a magnificently unchanged café and restaurant that has been a favorite with writers since it opened in 1839. Apparently, Queen Isabel II entertained her lovers in the upstairs dining room. ⏲ *20 min.*

3 ★ **Teatro de la Comedia.** When King Alfonso XII inaugurated the Teatro de la Comedia, with its wrought-iron twirls, at Calle Príncipe 14, in 1875, it was considered the most modern, beautiful, and

Teatro de la Comedia.

comfortable in the city. Now the seat of the Compañía Nacional de

Cervantes and *Don Quijote*

Don Quijote is possibly the most famous literary character in the world. The tale of the deluded knight, who with the help of his portly sidekick Sancho Panza tilted at windmills and sought the love of Dulcinea, is a much-loved classic. Miguel de Cervantes (1547–1616), the author of *Don Quijote*, led almost as exciting a life as his gangling knight, participating in great sea battles, being captured as a slave, and returning to Spain only to spend years in debtor's prison. International recognition (although little financial reward) came with the publication of *Don Quijote* in 1605, and Cervantes was broke once again when he died in 1616.

Teatro Clásico, who stage excellent Spanish classical drama, it is currently closed for refurbishment. (The theater company is temporarily based at the Teatre Pavón, Arts & Entertainment). ⏱ *10 min.*

④ ★★ **Teatro Español.** The Teatro Español is the city's most historic theater, which has its origins in a 16th-century corral, although the current building dates back only to 1807. Many great Spanish masterpieces have had their premier in this theater, including Lorca's *Yerma*, which opened here in 1934 (and was terribly received). ⏱ *10 min. Cl Príncipe 35.* ☎ *91-360-14-84. Metro: Sol.*

⑤ ★★ **kids** **Plaza Santa Ana.** The heart of the Barrio de las Letras neighborhood is the anarchic Plaza Santa Ana, crammed on all sides with bars and cafés. Kids squeal in the playgrounds, as their parents watch from the terrace cafés, and itinerant musicians make their

The Teatro Español is the city's most historic theater.

beady-eyed way from tourist to tourist. ⏱ *30 min. Metro: Sol.*

⑥ **La Suiza.** Established in 1858, this atmospheric *pastissería* combines shop and café and has a fabulous terrace out onto the square. Go for the mouthwatering cream-filled or fruit-topped pastries. *Plaza Santa Ana 2.* ☎ *91-521-08-11. $.*

⑦ **Ateneo Artístico, Cientifico y Literario.** Taking the Calle Prado down from the Plaza Santa Ana, you come to the Ateneo at No. 21. This venerable institution was founded in 1820 and established here since the 1930s to promote the study of arts and sciences. The gloriously old-fashioned library (not strictly open to the public, but the doorman might let you have a peek), with its glossy wooden stacks, remains a magnificent testament to Enlightenment-era ideals. ⏱ *10 min. C/ Prado 21. Metro: Antón Martín.*

⑧ **Site of Cervantes' House.** Take the Calle León to the corner of the Calle Cervantes. Very few places associated with poor Cervantes, now universally recognized as Spain's greatest writer, have survived the centuries. His modest home, which once stood here on a long-gone little square, was demolished in 1833, and a modest plaque is all that remains. ⏱ *10 min.*

⑨ ★★ **Casa-Museo Lope de Vega.** Lope de Vega (1562–1635) was a prolific dramatist, creating some of the greatest plays of the 16th-century. Here, in his charmingly restored home, he took refuge from his chaotic love life (two wives, several mistresses, and a spell in prison after being spurned by a pretty Madrileña called Elena Osirio), and churned out an immense body of work in his study. ⏱ *30 min. Cl Cervantes 11.* ☎ *91-429-92-16. Tues–Fri 9.30am–2pm & Sat 10am–2pm. Metro: Antón Martín.*

⑩ ★ Basilica Jesús de Medinaceli. Continue downhill to the bottom of the Calle Cervantes, and turn left to find the Basilica Jesús de Medinaceli. This church, completed in 1930, is dedicated to the protection of one of the most

statue. *C/ del Duque de Medinaceli s/n.* ☎ *91-364-40-50. Daily 8am–12.30pm & 6-9pm. Metro: Antón Martín.*

⑪ ★ Taberna la Dolores. Lavishly tiled, and resolutely old-fashioned, the Taberna de Dolores is a beacon of continuity in a *barrio* ruffled by change and gentrification. *Plaza de Jesús 4.* ☎ *91-429-22-43. $.*

Plaque commemorating Lope de Vega.

venerated statues in the city, the 17th-century Cristo de Medinaceli. According to legend, the statue was stolen by North African armies, who demanded a ransom equaling its weight in gold. However, when the statue was placed on the scales, it was found, miraculously, to weigh only as much as a single coin. During the Golden Age, the three most beautiful actresses (all named María) would attend Sunday mass in their finery, to the distraction of the congregation and the fury of the priest. Hundreds gather on Friday evenings to kiss the feet of the

⑫ ★ Convento de los Trinitariás. Turn right up the Calle Lope de Vega, and follow the forbidding stone wall of the Convento de los Trinitariás. Both Cervantes and Lope de Vega had daughters who became nuns here, and when Cervantes died, poverty stricken, in 1516, he was buried in the convent church. Unfortunately, his bones (like those of Lope de Vega) were lost, and his life is commemorated only by a large marble plaque on the wall. ⏱ *15 min. C/ Lope de Vega s/n. Metro: Antón Martín.*

Chueca & Malasaña Shopping & Nightlife

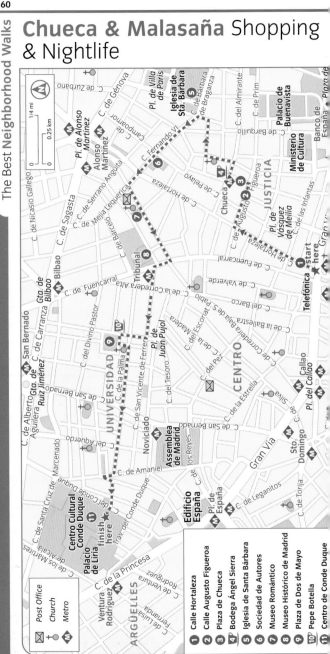

1 Calle Hortaleza
2 Calle Augusto Figueroa
3 Plaza de Chueca
4 Bodega Ángel Sierra
5 Iglesia de Santa Bárbara
6 Sociedad de Autores
7 Museo Romántico
8 Museo Histórico de Madrid
9 Plaza de Dos de Mayo
10 Pepe Botella
11 Centro de Conde Duque

Post Office
Church
Metro

The adjoining boho-chic neighborhoods of Chueca and Malasaña have boomed in recent years, although they remain appealingly scruffy around the edges. Chueca, the city's vibrant gay district, is sometimes called the 'SoHo of Madrid' and boasts designer fashion boutiques and restaurants, while Malasaña's numerous bars attract a young, alternative crowd. I think this walk is best in the late evening. START: **Metro to Gran Vía.**

1 ★ **Calle Hortaleza.** Calle Hortaleza is now Chueca's main shopping street, with scores of shops and cafés drawing a hip crowd looking for something different. I love the floaty dresses at H.A.N.D. (Have A Nice Day) at No. 26, and the hats at Cocoa (No. 28). Sleek designs for men and women can be found at Corleone's Company at No. 37, which showcases emerging Brazilian designers. ⏱ *20 min. Metro: Gran Vía.*

2 ★ **Calle Augusto Figueroa.** I love shoes and several designer outlet stores are clustered here, with a wide range of gorgeous shoes for men and women. Rummage for designs by Pura López, Farrutx, Dorotea, and Audley. ⏱ *30 min. Metro: Chueca.*

3 ★★ **Plaza de Chueca.** Calle Barbieri brings you to the heart of the neighborhood, the delightful Plaza de Chueca. Old-fashioned 1960s-style cafés rub up against

chic boutiques such as **L'Habilleur** at No. 8 (with designer bargains), all presided over by the historic, wood-paneled **Bodega Ángel Sierra** (this was masked by scaffolding at the time of writing). ⏱ *30 min. Metro: Chueca.*

4 ★★ **Bodega Ángel Sierra.** One of the oldest surviving taverns, this exquisite bodega is an obligatory stopping point in Chueca. I was brought here on one of my very first visits to the city, and the chilled vermouth and an anchovy wrapped around an olive remains a happy memory. *Cl Gravina, 11 Llibrería, 16.* ☎ *91-531-01-26. $.*

5 ★ **Iglesia de Santa Bárbara.** Wriggle up to the Plaza de Santa Bárbara, center of a smart residential neighborhood and quite different from the rest of Chueca. The splendid Baroque church once

Designer outlet stores on Calle Augusto Figueroa.

Bodega Ángel Sierra.

formed part of an immense monastery complex, established by Bárbara de Bragança (1711–1758), wife of Fernando VII (1713–1759), as a place of retreat in anticipation of her widowhood. However, she died before her husband, and both are buried in lavish marble tombs inside the church (which is open for mass only). The main monastery buildings now contain the **Tribunal Supremo** (the highest court in Spain). ⏱ 30 min. Cl Bárbara de Braganza 1–3. ☎ 91-319-48-11. Metro: Chueca or Colón.

6 ★★ **Sociedad de Autores.** Return to Calle Hortaleza along Calle Fernando VI to find the creamy **Palacio Longoria** (1902) decorated with icing-sugar swirls. This is the finest Modernista building in Madrid, and is home to the Society of Authors, which gathers royalties for Spanish writers. The palace is not open to the public, but you could try sweet-talking the doorman to let you look at the sweeping staircase. ⏱ 15 min. Cl Fernando VI 4. ☎ 91-349-95-50. Metro: Alonso Martínez.

7 ★ **Museo Romántico.** Set in an 18th-century palace, this museum contains an eccentric collection of 19th-century paintings, furnishings, books, and curiosities gathered by the museum's founder, the Marqués de Vega-Inclán. Closed indefinitely for restoration, you will have to content yourself with a glance at the handsome but rather worn exterior. ⏱ 15 min. Cl San Mateo 13. ☎ 91-448-01-63. http: museoromantico.mcu.es. Metro: Tribunal.

8 ★ **Museo Histórico de Madrid.** The 18th-century Hospital of San Fernando, now the city history museum, boasts a fabulous Churrigueresque doorway by Baroque architect Pedro de Ribera, encrusted with extravagant swirls

La Movida

When Franco died in 1975, ending 35 years of artistic repression Madrid's alternative cultural scene (particularly music, film, and fashion) exploded. Called 'La Movida', the movement peaked in the early 1980s, centered around Chueca. The old *barrio* was run-down and sleazy, populated with junkies, prostitutes, and elderly Madrileños too poor to leave, but it experienced a renaissance when artists poured in to take advantage of the cheap rents. By day the cracks still show, but at night, crowds of beautiful people emerge to enjoy the nightlife.

and is worth stopping by to see. The museum is currently undergoing a massive restoration and was closed at the time of writing. 🕐 *15 min. Cl Fuencarral 78. ☎ 91-701-18-63. www.munimadrid.es/museode historia. Metro: Tribunal.*

⑨ ★★ kids Plaza de Dos de Mayo. This is one of my favorite Madrileño squares. During the day, the split-level square is quiet—apart from the children in the little playground. By night, it's packed with young people, who fill the numerous bars clustered here. The name commemorates one of the most tragic events in Madrid's history, the massacre of the citizens by Napoleonic troops, which took place on May 2, 1808. A local seamstress, Manuel Malasaña, now a folk hero, was shot for defending herself with her scissors. The two army commanders who organized the revolt against the French, Daoíz and Velarde, are commemorated in a double statue. The archway behind them is all that remains of their barracks, which formerly occupied the square. 🕐 *10 min.*

Plaza de Dos de Mayo.

⑩ Pepe Botella. A classic on the corner of the Plaza Dos de Mayo, this shabby-chic café-bar is a big favorite with an alternative, arty crowd of actors, film directors, and writers. It's a mellow spot for a coffee during the day, but gets very lively at night. *Cl San Andrés 9. ☎ 91-522-43-09. $.*

⑪ ★ Centro de Conde Duque. An immense red-brick edifice with a lavish baroque portal, this was built in 1717 to house the Royal Guards. Now it's an important cultural institution, with a wide-ranging program of art exhibitions, music concerts, and flamenco festivals. It also houses the city's interesting collection of contemporary art. The surrounding streets are packed with arty cafés and bars. 🕐 *1 hr. Cl Conde Duque 11. ☎ 91-588-58-34. Museum open Tues–Sat 10am–2pm and 6–9pm, Sun and public hols 10.30am–2pm. www.munimadrid.es/ condeduque. Metro: Ventura Rodriguez.*

La Latina **& Lavapiés**

1. Plaza Tirso de Molina
2. Colegiata de San Isidro
3. Mercado de la Cebada
4. Plaza de la Humilladero
5. Capilla de San Isidro
6. Museo Orígenes (Casa San Isidro)
7. Casa Antonio
8. Basilica de San Francisco el Grande
9. Iglesia Virgen de la Paloma
10. El Rastro (C. Ribera de Curtidores)
11. La Corrala
12. Plaza Lavapiés

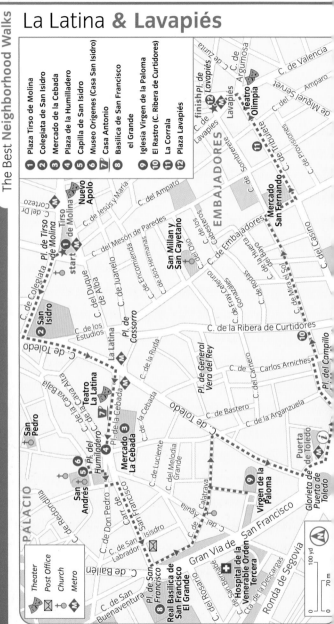

The ramshackle neighborhoods of La Latina and Lavapiés sprawl downhill from the grandiose Plaza Mayor. Traditionally occupied by the city's poorest, today the areas are popular and multicultural—if still run-down in places. Gentrification has taken hold of La Latina, where many of the city's best tapas bars are concentrated, and Lavapiés is now home to a new surge of immigrants, particularly Chinese and North Africans. START: **Metro to Tirso de Molina.**

① ★ kids **Plaza Tirso de Molina.** People used to scuttle quickly through this square, hoping to avoid unsavory characters. Now remodeled, local children play in the playground as their parents watch from the terrace cafés, and flower-sellers operate from modern wood-and-steel cabins. On summer evenings, there's barely a seat to be found. It's named after the Golden Age dramatist, Tirso de Molina (1583–1648), whose statue survived the renovations. 🕑 *20 min. Metro: Tirso de Molina.*

② ★ **Colegiata de San Isidro.** A short stroll west will bring you to the Calle Toledo, and the huge, gloomy Colegiata de San Isidro. This was built by the Jesuits in the 17th century but, after they were expelled from Spain in 1767, the church was revamped and rededicated to the city's patron saint, San Isidro, and his wife. Their remains are displayed in elaborate urns in the main altar. 🕑 *20 min. Cl Toledo 37.* ☎ *91-364-40-50. Open for mass only. Metro: La Latina.*

③ ★★ **Mercado de la Cebada.** I think this is the best central produce market in Madrid, with a wonderful range of top-quality fruit, vegetables, fresh fish, and meat. The 1960s-style grimy, gray exterior may not appeal to many, but I like its smooth, curving lines. 🕑 *40 min. Plaza Cebada s/n.* ☎ *91-365-91-76.*

Mercado de la Cebada.

Mon–Sat 8.30am–2.30pm and 5.30–8.30pm. Metro: La Latina.

④ ★ Plaza de la Humilladero. Just beyond the Market, the street widens into the popular Plaza de la Humilladero, smack at the center of one of the city's most celebrated tapas bar zones. See Tapas Tour (see p 52). ⏱ *20 min. Metro: La Latina.*

⑤ ★★ Capilla de San Isidro. A sumptuous baroque confection topped with a dome, this was built in the late 17th century to contain the bones of Madrid's beloved patron saint, San Isidro (later transferred to the Colegiata de San Isidro, see p 65). Badly damaged during the Civil War, it has now been immaculately restored. ⏱ *30 min. Plaza San Andrés 1.* ☎ *91-365-48-71. Mon–Thurs and Sat 8am–1pm and 6–8pm. Free admission. Metro: La Latina.*

⑥ ★ Museo Orígenes (Casa San Isidro). The Museum of Origins offers an interesting glimpse into Madrid's early history, with old plans, photographs, paintings, and archaeological finds. ⏱ *30 min. Plaza San Andrés 2.* ☎ *91-366-74-*

15. Tues–Fri 9.30am–8pm, Sat–Sun 10am–2pm. Aug Tues–Fri 9.30am–2.30pm, Sat–Sun 10am–2pm. Free admission. Metro: La Latina.

⑦ ★ Casa Antonio. This low-key tapas bar is usually busy thanks to the atmosphere and low prices. Don't miss the *croquetas. Plaza de la Cebada, 12. no phone. $.*

⑧ ★★ Basílica de San Francisco el Grande. At the end of the C/ San Francisco looms the vast neoclassical Basílica de San Francisco el Grande, erected at the end of the 18th century, and substantially renovated in the late 19th century. Despite royal protection and even a short-lived stint as pantheon for great Spaniards, the great Basilica is now best known for its lavish decoration and an early painting by Goya in a side chapel. A small (and frankly dull) museum contains a collection of religious art: I think the dahlia gardens next to it are much nicer. ⏱ *30 min. Plaza San Francisco 11.* ☎ *91-365-38-00. Tues–Sat 11.15am–12.45pm and 5.15–7pm. Admission 3€ adults. Metro: La Latina.*

Plenty of tapas options at the Plaza de la Humilladero.

El Rastro, Calle Ribera de Curtidores.

9 ★ **Iglesia Virgen de la Paloma.** Take Calle Calatrava to reach the Iglesia Virgen de la Paloma, the spiritual heart of La Latina and home to a much venerated 18th-century painting of the Virgin. The annual festival held in her honor (August 15) is a very touching affair, with a solemn parade followed by a huge street party. ⏱ *30 min. Plaza Virgen de la Paloma.* ☎ *91-365-46-69. Tues–Sat 11.15am–12.45pm and 5.15–7pm. Admission 3€. Metro: La Latina.*

10 ★★★ **El Rastro (Calle Ribera de Curtidores).** Madrid's celebrated flea market, El Rastro, dates back to the Middle Ages. It takes place on the steep Calle Ribera de Curtidores every Sunday morning, attracting a huge crowd of locals, tourists—and those who prey on them. Keep a very close eye on your belongings. It's a colorful spectacle, with stalls selling everything from car parts to antiques, African crafts to Asian jewelry. The market runs down at around 2 or 3pm, when everyone heads to the tapas bars around the Plaza Humilladero (see above). ⏱ *1 hr. Cl Ribera de Curtidores and surrounding streets. Market held Sunday mornings. Metro: Puerta de Toledo or La Latina.*

11 **La Corrala.** A century or so ago, these neighborhoods were filled with corralas, humble timber-framed apartment blocks set around a courtyard, in which the poor were crammed in cramped conditions. Few have survived, but this one was renovated in the late 1970s and still occasionally provides an unusual setting for flamenco concerts or other events. Another corrala, at Calle Carlos Arniches 3–5, is currently being redeveloped and will eventually house a new museum. ⏱ *10 min. Cl del Mesón de Paredes, between Cl Tribulete and Cl Sombrerete.*

12 ★ **Plaza Lavapiés.** Once the heart of the Jewish ghetto, before the expulsion of the Jews from Spain in 1492, the Plaza Lavapiés is now the center of Madrid's most multi-cultural barrio. Just as in the past, when these barrios bajos ('low neighborhoods') were home to immigrants from the rest of Spain, hoping to find work and a chance for a better life, so now they are home to immigrants from farther afield. In fact, it's estimated that about 50 per cent of the residents of Lavapiés were born outside Spain. ⏱ *15 min. Metro: Lavapiés.*

Traditional **Madrid**

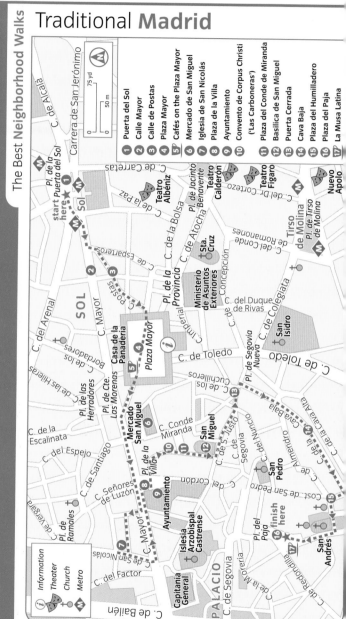

1 Puerta del Sol
2 Calle Mayor
3 Calle de Postas
4 Plaza Mayor
5 Cafés on the Plaza Mayor
6 Mercado de San Miguel
7 Iglesia de San Nicolas
8 Plaza de la Villa
9 Ayuntamiento
10 Convento de Corpus Christi ('Las Carboneras')
11 Plaza del Conde de Miranda
12 Basilica de San Miguel
13 Puerta Cerrada
14 Cava Baja
15 Plaza del Humilladero
16 Plaza del Paja
17 La Musa Latina

The old heart of Madrid is an atmospheric maze of narrow streets, secret squares, and beautiful churches. This tour meanders through the ancient core, taking in some well-known monuments such as the magnificent Plaza Mayor and lingering in secluded corners off the beaten track. START: **Metro to Sol.**

1 ★★ **Puerta del Sol.** During the 16th century, visitors to the newly established Spanish capital gathered at one of three meeting places: the Puerta del Sol (the main gate to the east of the city); the Plaza Mayor; and the Plaza de la Villa. Our visit will begin at the first of these (we'll visit the other two later). For description, see p 15. ⏲ *30 min. Metro: Sol.*

2 ★ **Calle Mayor.** This was, as its name suggests, the main street of the old city, linking the Puerta del Sol with the Plaza Mayor. Although long eclipsed by modern avenues such as the Gran Vía, it's still full of life. ⏲ *20 min. Metro: Sol.*

3 ★ **Calle de Postas.** Plunge into old Madrid via the ancient Calle de Postas. Despite the souvenir

shops and tourists—or because of the carnival atmosphere they evoke—this attractive, semi-pedestrianized street manages to retain a strong flavor of the past. It's named for the first post office, which stood here until it was moved to the Puerta del Sol in the 18th century. **The Posada del Peine**, now a boutique hotel, has occupied the same building at No. 17 for almost four centuries, making it one of the oldest here. ⏲ *20 min. Metro: Sol.*

4 ★★★ kids **Plaza Mayor.** The immense Plaza Mayor is completely enclosed by handsome baroque buildings, with access to the central square provided by several archways. After admiring the square (for description, see p 39), leave by the northern side back to the Calle Mayor. ⏲ *40 min. Metro: Sol.*

Attractive street sign on Calle Mayor.

CALLE
MAYOR

Plaza Mayor.

5 Cafés on the Plaza Mayor.
Take your pick of several cafés on the Plaza Mayor, most of which boast great terraces. If you want to blend in with the locals, pick one in the shade. Or join the pink-faced northern European tourists and soak up the sun.

6 Mercado de San Miguel.
Alongside the Plaza Mayor, on little Plaza de San Miguel is the elegant Mercado de San Miguel. This glass-and-steel market was erected

between 1913 and 1916 to designs that took their inspiration from the Les Halles in Paris, and it is the only surviving historic market of its kind in Madrid. After years of decline, it was recently bought by a private consortium, which hopes to create a gastronomic center to rival Barcelona's famous La Boquería market. ⏱ *10 min. Plaza San Miguel s/n. www.mercadodesan miguel.es Metro: Sol.*

7 ★★ Iglesia de San Nicolás.
Continue almost to the end of Calle Mayor and walk up Calle Nicolás to the city's oldest church. The lovely Iglesia de San Nicolás was built over the ruins of a former mosque in the 12th century, when the pretty brick minaret was preserved to form a steeple. *Plaza San Nicolás 48. ☎ 91-369-05-79. Open for mass only. Metro: Ópera.*

8 ★★★ Plaza de la Villa. Return to the Calle Mayor and the Plaza de la Villa, a tiny square that is easy to overlook but contains a fascinating ensemble of fine buildings. On the left is the **Torre de los Lujanes**, with its sturdy square tower and

The Plaza de la Villa contains an ensemble of fine buildings.

Take a tour to view the City Hall's impressive baroque ceilings.

cream stripes. This is the oldest palace in the city, built during the 15th century, and where, so legend has it, Francis I of France was kept prisoner until a ransom was raised. Opposite is the handsome **Casa de la Villa** (City Hall, see below ⑨). The third building is the **Casa de Cisneros**, a graceful 16th-century palace with Plateresque decoration—and the palace I'd buy if I were a millionaire. ⏱ *30 min. Plaza de la Villa. Metro: Ópera or Sol.*

⑨ ★★ **Ayuntamiento.** The Casa de la Villa (City Hall) was completed at the end of the 17th century and endowed with some flamboyant baroque flourishes including elaborate doorways. Unfortunately, very little of the original interior has survived, and, to my great disappointment, Madrid's City Hall is almost as dull inside as you would expect a municipal office to be (the tourist office runs tours on Monday afternoons; book in advance). However, the tour does take in three extraordinary rooms: the resplendent **Salón de Recepciones,** with an exquisitely painted baroque ceiling; the original **patio**, now covered with a stained-glass ceiling in jewel-colored tones; and the 19th-century **Salón de Plenos**, a riot of red velvet and gilt. ⏱ *1 hr. Plaza de la*

Villa. Book tours, which take place Mon at 5pm, through the tourist office, Tours in English and Spanish. Free admission. Metro: Ópera or Sol.

⑩ ★ **Convento de Corpus Christi ('Las Carboneras').** Tucked around the corner from the Plaza de la Villa, if you take the narrow passage next to the Torre de los Lujanes, is a wonderful time-capsule convent. You can enter the silent church for a moment's contemplation, or pick up some of the nuns' handmade sweet treats by ringing the doorbell. In ancient tradition, the sweets are delivered through a revolving drawer into which you put your money. ⏱ *20 min.* ☎ *93-476-57-21. Sweets sold 9.30am–1pm & 4–6.30pm. Metro: Ópera.*

⑪ **Plaza del Conde de Miranda.** This charming little square is one of the oldest in the city, flanked by the Convent de las Carboneras (see ⑩ above) and the Basílica de San Andrés (see ⑫ below). In summer, there's an art market at weekends. ⏱ *10 min. Plaza del Conde de Miranda 3. Metro: Ópera.*

⑫ **Basílica de San Miguel.** This impressive 18th-century basilica stands on a site once occupied by a Romanesque church dedicated to

Capilla del Obispo in the Plaza del Paja.

Justo and Pastor, two children martyred by the Romans. Although it was rededicated to San Miguel, the façade still bears carvings depicting the murdered children. 🕐 *20 min. Cl de San Justo 4. Free admission. Mon–Sat 10.30am–12.30pm, 7–8.30pm; Sun 9.45am–1.45pm, 6.30–9pm. Metro: Ópera.*

🔞 Puerta Cerrada. The Puerta Cerrada gets its curious name ('closed door') from the medieval gateway to the city which stood on this spot until the end of the 16th century, when the early medieval walls were pulled down. Thieves, pickpockets, and delinquents of all kinds used to lurk in the shadows, ready to prey on all those who entered: as a consequence, the gate was usually locked. Now the square is little more than a confluence of streets, but several of the alleys that splinter off here are lined with good restaurants and bars. Heading up towards the Plaza Mayor, the **Calle de Cuchilleros** ('Street of the Knife-sharpeners') is always animated

and busy, and the **Cava Baja** (see p 52), which leads downhill, almost certainly has more tapas bars per meter than anywhere else in the city. 🕐 *10 min. Metro: La Latina.*

🔞 ★★ Cava Baja. Take this ancient bar-lined street to reach the next stop on the tour. For tips on bars, see the Tapas Tour (p 52).

🔞 ★★ Plaza del Humilladero. The focus of the obligatory post-Rastro tapas crawl, this square is surrounded by great tapas bars. According to local tradition, it is where the city's patron saint once lived (his former home is now the Museo Orígenes, see p 66). Next door, the pretty baroque Capilla de San Isidro was built to contain the saint's apparently uncorrupted remains (see p 66). 🕐 *40 min. Metro: La Latina.*

🔞 ★★ Plaza del Paja. Duck around the back of the Plaza del Humilladero to find the Plaza del Paja, a beautiful square currently marred by the scaffolding that surrounds the great, domed **Capilla del Obispo**. The 'Bishop's Chapel' is reputedly one of the finest Renaissance churches in the city—but it's been closed for so long that I've never managed to see the interior. When the renovation is finally completed, visit the splendid marble tombs of Don Francisco de Vargas, councilor to Ferdinand and Isabella, and his family. 🕐 *30 min. Metro: La Latina.*

🔞 La Musa Latina. This is a favorite of mine in the Plaza de la Paja. The designer tapas are mouth-watering, and the artistic crowd is fun and friendly. I prefer it in the early evening: later, it gets packed and service can be achingly slow. *Costanilla de San Andrés 12. ☎ 91-354-02-55. $$.* ●

Madrid Shopping

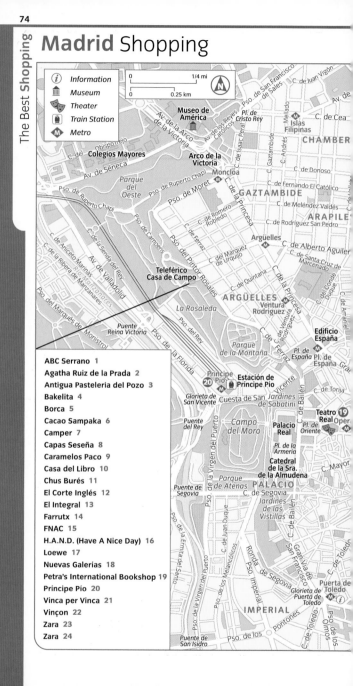

Legend:
- ⓘ Information
- 🏛 Museum
- 🎭 Theater
- 🚉 Train Station
- Ⓜ Metro

Shopping Best Bets

Best for **Rummaging for Antiques**
★★ Nuevas Galerías, *C/ Ribera de Curtidores 12 (p 77)*

Best **Affordable Designer Clothing**
★★ El Integral, *C/ León 25 (p 79)*

Best Place for **Impulse Buys You Won't Regret (Women)**
★★ El Integral, *C/ Hortaleza 26 (p 79)*

Best **Luxury Leather Goods**
★ Loewe, *C/ Serrano 26 (p 79)*

Best Shop for **Slaves to Design**
★★ Vinçon, *C/ Castelló 18 (p 78)*

Best **Vintage Cool**
★ Bakelita, *C/ Cervantes 26 (p 78)*

Best **Designer Chocolates**
★ Cacao Sampaka, *C/ Orellana 4 (p 80)*

Best **Traditional Garment Shop**
★ Capas Seseña, *C/ de la Cruz 23 1 (p 80)*

Best **Secondhand Bookshop Named for a Cat**
★★ Petra's International Bookshop, *C/ Campomanes 13 (p 77)*

Best **High-street Bookshop**
★ Casa del Libro, *Gran Via 29 (p 77)*

Best **One-Stop Shopping**
Príncipe Pío, *Paseo de la Florida s/n (p 78)*

Best **Flea Market**
El Rastro, *C/ Ribera de Curtidores (p 67)*

Most **Theatrical Boutique**
★ Agatha Ruiz de la Prada, *C/ Serrano 27 (p 78)*

Best **Floor-to-Ceiling Candy**
★★ Caramelos Paco, *C/ Toledo 53–55 (p 80)*

Best **Celebrity Jeweler**
★★ Chus Burés, *C/ Claudio Coello 88 (p 80)*

Best **Pointy Shoes**
★★ Farrutx, *C/ Serrano 7 (p 80)*

Metal robot toys at El Integral.

Madrid **Shopping A to Z**

Antiques & Art
★ **Nuevas Galerías** CENTRAL
MADRID   This street is best known
for the Rastro flea market, held here
every Sunday, but it's also home to
the city's best antique shops. Several are gathered in the atmospheric
Nuevas Galerías, where 60 individual
and unique shops are arranged
around a courtyard. There's a huge
range of antiques, bric-a-brac, and
objets d'art. *C/ Ribera de Curtidores
12.* ☎ *91-520-56-53. Metro: La
Latina. Map p 74.*

Books & Music
★ **Casa del Libro** CENTRAL
MADRID   This enormous bookstore
has a good international section,
with a wide range of travel guides
and maps for visitors. *Gran Vía 29.*
☎ *91-521-21-13. www.casaddelli
libro.com. MC, V. Metro: Gran Vía.
Map p 74.*

FNAC CENTRAL MADRID   The
FNAC megastore is mostly main-
stream books and music, with a
decent selection of flamenco and
other Spanish music. It also sells
electronic goods from computers
to cameras. *C/ Preciados 28.*

Find English secondhand books at Petra's.

☎ *91-595-62-00. AE, DC, MC, V.
Metro: Gran Vía. Map p 74.*

★★ **Petra's International
Bookshop** CENTRAL MADRID
A tiny doorway leads into this marvelous secondhand bookshop
(named after the American owner's
cat), with a huge selection of books
in English and other languages.

Prime Shopping Zones

For all the best high-street chains, saunter down the **Gran Vía**.
The pedestrianized **Calle Preciados**, which links the Gran Vía with
the Puerta del Sol, has the big department store El Corte Inglés and
a huge FNAC. The most upmarket shopping neighborhood by far is
Salamanca, with Gucci, Chanel, and others gathered around the
Calle Serrano. For funky, offbeat fashion, try Chueca, particularly
the **Calle Hortaleza**, and increasingly, the small streets around the
Plaza Santa Ana. The Sunday morning flea market, **El Rastro**, has
been a Madrid tradition for hundreds of years.

The Best Shopping

C/ Campomanes 13. ☎ 91-541-72-91. No credit cards. Metro: Ópera or Santo Domingo. Map p 74.

Department Stores/Shopping Centers

★ ABC Serrano CENTRAL MADRID

A smart shopping center in the chi-chi Salamanca neighborhood, this is set in the lavishly tiled former ABC newspaper building. The smart shops and the good rooftop restaurant with a fabulous terrace make it popular with ladies who lunch and business people. C/ Serrano 61 (C/ Castellana 34). ☎ 91-577-50-31. www.abcserrano.com. AE, DC, MC, V. Metro: Núñez de Balboa, or Serrano. Map p 74.

★ El Corte Inglés CENTRAL

Spain's largest department store chain sells everything from wine to furniture. You'll also find a restaurant, travel agent, and excellent grocery store. C/ Preciados 3. ☎ 91-379-80-00. www.elcorteingles.es. AE, DC, MC, V. Metro: Callao. Map p 74.

★ Príncipe Pío CENTRAL MADRID

I don't generally enjoy shopping malls, but this one is set in a beautifully converted 19th-century train

Príncipe Pío is set in a 19th-century converted train station.

station, and is attractively light and airy. All the most popular fashion chains can be found here (Zara, Mango, H&M), plus several good shoe shops. Probably my favorite for one-stop shopping. Paseo de la Florida s/n. ☎ 91-758-00-40. www.ccprincipepio.com. Metro: Príncipe Pío. Map p 74.

Designer Home Goods & Furnishings

★ Bakelita CENTRAL MADRID

A very stylish shop selling classic vintage furnishings and objets d'art from the 20th century. Although some pieces have price tags that will make you gasp, there are some more affordable objects, which make really special gifts. C/ Cervantes 26. ☎ 91-429-23-87. www.bakelita.com. AE, DC, MC, V. Metro: Sol. Map p 74.

★★ Vinçon CENTRAL MADRID

A magnificent contemporary design emporium with everything from furnishings to kitchen goods, including lighting, children's toys, and even the coolest, retro-chic scooter helmets in the city. Prices range from jaw-dropping to surprisingly affordable. C/ Castelló 18. ☎ 91-578-05-20. www.vincon.com. AE, DC, MC, V. Metro: Velázquez. Map p 74.

★ Zara CENTRAL MADRID

The fashion phenomenon Zara has a fabulous range of affordable interior design, with bedding, lamps, and soft furnishings. This is the biggest Zara Home store in the city, with a special section for Zara Kids Home. C/ Serrano 88. ☎ 900-900-314. AE, DC, MC, V. Metro: Rubén Darío. Map p 74.

Fashion & Accessories

★ Agatha Ruiz de la Prada SALAMANCA

The bright, bold designs of Agatha Ruiz de la Prada look like something a child would

Stylish vintage furnishing at Bakelita.

create. This crazy store with its clashing colors and contrasting patterns has a little bit of everything, from adult fashion to fabrics and goods for the home. I prefer the children's clothes, which are fun and original. *C/ Serrano 27.* ☎ *93-319-05-51. AE, MC, V. Metro: Serrano. Map p 74.*

★★ **El Integral** CENTRAL MADRID This funky little boutique, located in an old bakery, sells a great selection of fun, retro-chic fashion, accessories, underwear, costume jewelry, stationery, and decorative objects. Bright colors and cool design are key, and I often come here to pick up gifts for friends. *C/ León 25.* ☎ *91-429-16-18. AE, MC, V. Metro: Antón Martin. Map p 74.*

★★ **H.A.N.D. (Have A Nice Day)** CENTRAL MADRID I defy anyone to leave empty-handed from this hip, relaxed boutique—the dresses, jackets, and tops are quite irresistible. Spanish actress Paz Vega is one of H.A.N.D.'s many fans. *C/ Hortaleza 26.* ☎ *91-429-16-18. AE, MC, V. Metro: Antón Martin. Map p 74.*

★ **Loewe** SALAMANCA This is probably the most luxurious of the upmarket Spanish designers. It started out in leather goods—and the shoes and bags are still gorgeous and highly desirable—but has branched into high fashion in recent years. *C/ Serrano 26.* ☎ *91-577-60-56. www.loewe.es. AE, MC, V. Metro: Serrano. Map p 74.*

★ **Zara** CENTRAL MADRID Zara is an internationally successful Spanish fashion chain, which offers catwalk styles for budget-conscious men, women, and kids. *C/ Preciados 18.* ☎ *91-521-09-58. www.zara.es. AE, DC, MC, V. Metro: Gran Vía. Map p 74.*

Flowers

★★ **Vinca per Vinca.** CENTRAL MADRID A tiny florist in the fashionable Santa Ana neighborhood, with a hot-pink façade, lush plants, and luscious blooms arranged in original bouquets. *C/ Lope de Vega 12.* ☎ *91-156-82-23. MC, V .Metro: Antón Martín. Map p 74.*

Food & Drink

★ **Antigua Pasteleria del Pozo** CENTRAL MADRID This splendid pastry shop opened its doors in

Hip boutique H.A.N.D.

1830 and has been making the tastiest traditional treats in the city ever since. The handmade cream pastries are my favorite. Purchases are rung up on an antique cash register. *C/ del Pozo 8.* ☎ *91-522-38-94. MC, V. Metro: Sevilla. Map p 74.*

★ **Cacao Sampaka** L'EIXAMPLE These rich designer chocolates come in unusual flavors (try them with cinnamon or rose petals), and are sleekly packaged to make great gifts. There's a café attached, where you can tuck into thick hot chocolate and mouthwatering pastries. *C/ Orellana 4.* ☎ *93-319-58-40. AE, DC, MC, V. Metro: Alonso Martínez. Map p 74.*

★ **Caramelos Paco** L'EIXAMPLE Every kid's dream—and their parents' worst nightmare. This delightfully old-fashioned sweetshop was established in 1936, and is a magical world of floor-to-ceiling candy. Its bonbon-packed windows have become a city icon. *C/ Toledo 53–55.* ☎ *91-365-42-58. www.caramelos paco.com. MC, V. Metro: Alonso Martínez. Map p 74.*

Gifts & Souvenirs
★ **Borca** CENTRAL MADRID This shop specializes in hand-embroidery. The exquisite *mantillas* (the classic Spanish fringed shawl) are beautiful, and better value here than in tourist-oriented gift shops. They also have hand-embroidered tablecloths and bed linen. A little Spanish will go a long way here, so bring your phrase book. *C/ del Marqués Viudo de Portejos 2.* ☎ *91-523-61-53. AE, DC, MC, V. Metro: Sol. Map p 74.*

★ **Capas Seseña** CENTRAL MADRID A classic in Madrid, and worth a visit even if you only want to browse. Seseña specializes in the dignified Spanish cape, available in several styles including updated versions for the 21st century. Camilo José Cela wore a cape from this shop when he was awarded the Novel prize for literature, and photos in the window show bigwigs such as Hilary Clinton swathed in elegant folds. *C/ de la Cruz 23.* ☎ *91-531-68-40. AE, MC, V. Metro: Sol. Map p 74.*

Jewelry
★★ **Chus Burés** CENTRAL MADRID Jewelry designer to the stars, Chus Burés creates striking, original pieces, which are displayed in his bold, red-and-black showroom. Stunning and eye-catching, but with a hefty price tag. *C/ Claudio Coello 88.* ☎ *91-576-39-01. www.chusbures.com. AE, DC, MC, V. Metro: Núñez de Balboa. Map p 74.*

Shoes
★ **Camper** EL RAVAL Camper shoes, originally from Mallorca, are now famous around the world. The quirky and original designs for men and women meld style with comfort, and have become very hip in recent years. This is just one of several branches around the city. *Gran Vía 54.* ☎ *91-547-52-34. www.camper.es. AE, DC, MC, V. Metro: Gran Vía. Map p 74.*

★ **Farrutx** CENTRAL MADRID Exclusive leather goods—shoes, bags, wallets, belts—for vampish It-girls and style-conscious men. Prices are very reasonable for the quality on offer, but I still sneak off to their sale shop (at Calle Augusto Figueroa 18, in Chueca) to rummage for bargains. *C/ Serrano 7.* ☎ *91-576-94-93. www.farrutx.es. AE, DC, MC, V. Metro: Retiro. Map p 74.* ●

5 Madrid **Outdoors**

Real Jardín **Botánico de Madrid (Botanic Gardens)**

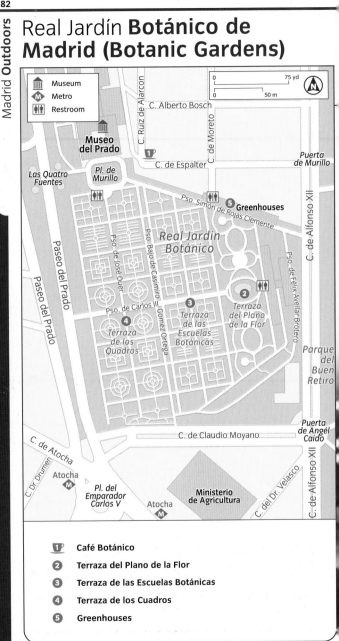

Museum
M Metro
Restroom

Museo del Prado
C. Ruiz de Alarcon
C. Alberto Bosch
C. de Moreto
Puerta de Murillo
C. de Espalter

Las Quatro Fuentes
Pl. de Murillo

Paseo del Prado

Pso. Simón de Rojas Clemente
5 Greenhouses

Real Jardín Botánico

C. de Alfonso XII

Pso. de José Quer
Pso. Bajo de Casimiro Gómez Ortega

Pso. de Félix Avelar Brotero

Pso. de Carlos III

3 Terraza de las Escuelas Botánicas

2 Terraza del Plano de la Flor

4 Terraza de los Quadros

Parque del Buen Retiro

C. de Claudio Moyano

Puerta de Angél Caído

C. de Atocha
C. de Drumen

Atocha M

Pl. del Emparador Carlos V

Atocha M

Ministerio de Agricultura

C. del Dr. Velasco

C. de Alfonso XII

1 Café Botánico

2 Terraza del Plano de la Flor

3 Terraza de las Escuelas Botánicas

4 Terraza de los Cuadros

5 Greenhouses

Step out of the hurly burly of the city into these beautiful botanic gardens, where birdsong keeps the hum of traffic at bay. Established in 1755, they are laid out in a series of elegant baroque terraces and are particularly inviting in spring, when the flowers come into bloom, and in autumn, when the leaves change color.

START: **Metro to Banco de España.**

1 **Café Botánico.** Just around the corner from the entrance to the Botanic Gardens, this old-fashioned café is ideal for a coffee. *C/ Ruiz de Alarcón 27.* ☎ *91-420-23-42. $.*

2 ★ **Terraza del Plano de la Flor.** The uppermost terrace, nearest the entrance, is shaded by palms and other trees, with velvety grass fringed with clipped hedges and a charming pond.

3 ★ **Terraza de las Escuelas Botánicas.** Divided into 12 sections, neatly hedged, and carefully arranged around a dozen stone fountains, the second terrace resembles a baroque *parterre*. A dizzying range of plants are found here, carefully grouped according to their family, and labeled in accordance with their original function—teaching botany.

4 ★★ **Terraza de los Cuadros.** The lowest terrace is also the largest, with ornamental plants, a beautiful rose garden (in bloom from late-May to mid-June), and—one of my favorites—a section dedicated to medicinal plants. This part of the garden is where

The peaceful Real Jardín Botánico de Madrid.

Madrileños come to hide themselves away and enjoy a discreet picnic.

5 ★ **Greenhouses.** Back on the top terrace are the three main greenhouses. The oldest is the graceful 18th-century **Pabellón Villanueva**, used for temporary exhibitions. The 19th-century **Graells Greenhouse** is hot and steamy, and contains tropical and aquatic plants including enormous water lilies. The **Exhibition Greenhouse** is dedicated to plants from three different climate types: tropical, temperate, and desert.

Practical Matters: Botanic Gardens

Plaza de Murillo 1. ☎ 91-420-30-17. www.rjb.csic.es. Admission 2€ adults, 1€ students, free for under-10s. Metro Atocha.

Casa **de Campo**

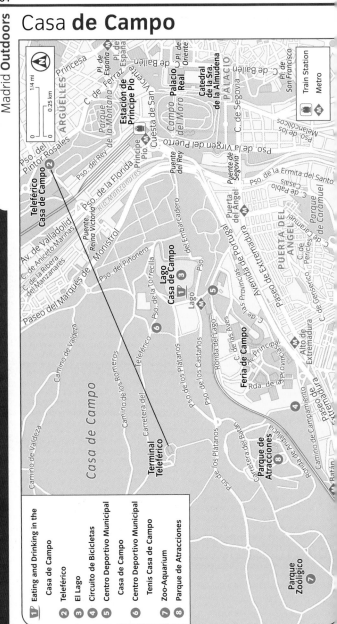

Eating and Drinking in the
  Casa de Campo
2 Teleférico
3 El Lago
4 Circuito de Bicicletas
5 Centro Deportivo Municipal
  Casa de Campo
6 Centro Deportivo Municipal
  Tenis Casa de Campo
7 Zoo-Aquarium
8 Parque de Atracciones

The largest public park in the city, the vast **Casa del Campo** was once a royal hunting ground. Now it's semi-wild, and full of tree-shaded paths, perfect for quiet strolls or some mountain biking. There is also a very popular lake with boats for rent and sailing activities, as well as sports centers with pool and tennis courts, the large city zoo, and a fun park (Parque de Atracciones) full of thrilling rides. **START: Teleferico from Parque del Oeste to Casa de Campo, then 15-min walk. Or metro to Lago.**

1 **Eating and drinking in the Casa de Campo.** There are numerous fast-food options in the Casa de Campo, from the hot dogs available at the cable car station to the cafés in the zoo and funfair. There are restaurants for more substantial fare gathered near the lake, but generally prices are high and quality mediocre. I often prefer to pick up picnic supplies—from La Cebada market if I have time, or if not, at the convenient supermarket in El Corte Inglés (there's a branch at C/ de la Princesa 56, near the Argüelles metro stop).

2 ★★ kids **Teleférico.** The most entertaining way to reach the Casa del Campo is to take the cable car, which swings over the rooftops at the western end of the city and deposits visitors in the center of the park. Try to go on a clear day, when the views stretch all the way to the distant Sierras. It's easier, if rather less fun, to take the metro to the Lago stop if you want to head directly to the park information center. See p 48, Madrid for Kids.

3 ★ **El Lago.** In the southwest corner of the park is the large and extremely popular recreational lake. You can spot it from miles around, thanks to the huge, jetting fountain in the center, which spurts high into the air. There's a useful information center here, which can provide leaflets showing cycling and walking routes, as well as information on guided visits (currently in Spanish only). The city council has extensive plans for improvements to park services (ideas include a free bike hire service for getting around the park), and so it's a good idea to visit

Take the cable car to Casa de Campo.

The leafy Casa de Campo.

the information center and find out what's new. *Information center* ☎ *91-479-60-02. Open May–Sept 16 10am–2pm and 5–8pm, Sept 17–Apr 9am–2pm and 4–7pm. Metro: Lago.*

④ Circuito de Bicicletas. A special circuit, specifically tailored to the requirements of mountain-bikers, exists within the park. The route begins at the Puerta Dante, near the Batán metro stop, and takes in a large section of the wildest part of the park. It divides into two routes, but both are linked. The route is poorly signposted, and the surface frequently changes, from asphalt road to dirt track, so

take it slowly the first time you try it out. However, it is one of the few places to cycle in Madrid, which is surprisingly bicycle-unfriendly. *Information center* ☎ *91-479-60-02. For opening details see bullet* ③ *above.*

⑤ ★ Centro Deportivo Municipal Casa de Campo. This municipal sports center attracts a vast crowd in summer, when the indoor pool is closed and two outdoor pools are opened instead. There is also a children's pool, making this a huge favorite with Madrileño families. It's a shame that there isn't more grass and less cement, but the pools are nonetheless a boon in the searing

Bullfighters in the Casa del Campo

If you find yourself strolling through some of the quieter reaches of the Casa del Campo, you may come across a very curious sight: a group of adolescents very seriously twirling capes in slow, precise patterns. These are apprentice *toreros* (bullfighters) who attend the prestigious bullfighting school (Escuela Taurina de Madrid) located in the Casa del Campo. Although most of the students are male, a small percentage (roughly 10 per cent) is women. Even if, like me, you disagree with bullfighting, the sight of the slow, dance-like cape movements is mesmerizing.

summer heat. Other facilities include a gym and sauna, plus special activities and classes. *Paseo Puerta de Angel 7.* ☎ *91-463-00-50. Indoor pool open early-Sept–May Mon–Fri 9.45am–8pm, summer outdoor pools open daily 11am–9pm. Admission 4.20€ adults, 2.55€ under 18. Metro: Lago or Puerta del Ángel.*

⑥ Centro Deportivo Municipal Tenis Casa de Campo. Practice your backhand at this municipal sports center, with 15 outdoor courts. *Camino Principe 2.* ☎ *91-464-96-17. Hours vary; call in advance. Admission 5.40€ adults, 3.25€ under 18. Metro: Lago.*

⑦ Zoo-Aquarium. There are two attractions for the price of one at Madrid's city zoo, which also includes a surprisingly large aquarium section. All the usual favorites are here, from lions and tigers in the zoo to dolphins and penguins in the aquarium. The antics of the audience-loving dolphins (ask for times of shows at the entrance gate) are always hugely enjoyable—although surprisingly short at just 15 minutes. *Casa de Campo.* ☎ *91-512-37-70.*

Admission 17.90€ adults, 14.50€ children 3–7 and seniors, free for under-3s. Opening hours vary from week to week, but are roughly daily 11am–6pm in winter, 10.30am–7pm in summer, later at weekends. Check the website or ask at the tourist office before you visit. Closed Jan. Metro: Casa de Campo, or cable car and a 15-minute walk.

⑧ Parque de Atracciones. You can hear the whoops of delight from this theme park across half of the park. Thrill-seekers will get a rush from some of the scarier rides, which twist 360 degrees or plunge terrifyingly towards the earth, while the younger (and the more sedate) are well catered for with a host of enjoyable alternatives. *Casa de Campo.* ☎ *91-563-29-00. Admission (and unlimited rides) 27.50€ adults, 18€ children 3–6 and seniors, free for under-3s. Opening hours vary from week to week, but are roughly weekends only 12–7pm in winter, daily 12–8pm in summer, later at weekends. Check the website or ask at the tourist office before you visit. Metro: Casa de Campo, or cable car and a 15-minute walk.*

Entrance to Parque de Atracciones.

88

Madrid **Outdoors**

Parque **del Oeste**

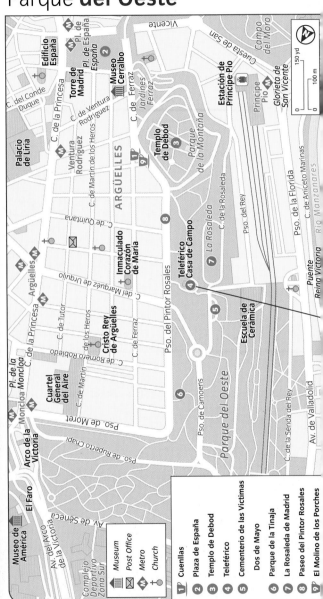

🏛	Museum
✉	Post Office
Ⓜ	Metro
✝	Church

1 Cuenllas
2 Plaza de España
3 Templo de Debod
4 Teleférico
5 Cementerio de las Víctimas Dos de Mayo
6 Parque de la Tinaja
7 La Rosaleda de Madrid
8 Paseo del Pintor Rosales
9 El Molino de los Porches

In the early 20th century, a civic-minded mayor oversaw the development of the undulating, green Parque del Oeste, providing the grateful Madrileños with their first, purpose-built public space for relaxation. Shaded with tall, leafy trees, the park is now perhaps best known for its magnificent rose garden, La Rosaleda, one of the finest in Spain. On summer evenings, the grassy banks fill up with picnickers who come to enjoy the views of the sun setting behind the distant Sierras. START: **Plaza de España.**

1 **Cuenllas.** If you're looking for some fancy picnic goodies to take into the park, Cuenllas is the answer. Linked to a prestigious restaurant (on the same street at No. 5), this sells an impressive range of cheeses, wines, oils, spreads, and all kinds of delicious gourmet food-stuffs. *C/ Ferraz 3.* ☎ *91-547-31-33. Metro: Ventura Rodríguez. $$.*

2 **Plaza de España.** The metro will bring you out on this large, celebrated, and extraordinarily dull city square. After a quick look at the bronze statues of Don Quijote and Sancho Panza, stride across the square towards the shimmering Templo de Debod, just visible in the corner of the Parque del Oeste. *Metro: Plaza España.*

3 ★ **Templo de Debod.** This 4th-century BC Egyptian temple once stood on the banks of the Nile, and its serene beauty stands in marked contrast to the ugly modern development around the nearby Plaza de España. Fortunately, the gardens in which it sits mark the entrance to the Parque del Oeste, keeping the eyesore apartment blocks at bay. The classic view of the temple, with the huge skies of Madrid stretching behind it, is one of the most amazing spectacles in the city. For description, see Madrid's Quirky Museums, p 44. *C/ Ferraz 1.* ☎ *91-366-74-15. Admission free. Oct–Mar Tues–Fri 9.45am– 1.45pm and 4.15–6.15pm, Sat–Sun 10am–2pm; Apr–Sept Tues–Fri 10am– 2pm and 6–8pm, Sat–Sun 10am– 2pm. Free guided visits for families (in Spanish) first Sat of every month (except Aug) at 11.30am and 12.30pm. Metro: Plaza de España or Ventura Rodríguez.*

4 ★★ kids **Teleférico.** Madrid's enjoyable cable car sways across the western end of the city into the

Templo de Debod.

A water feature on Parque del Oeste.

huge expanse of the Casa del Campo park from the cable car station in the center of the Parque del Oeste. See p 18, the Best in Three Days.

5 ★ **Cementerio de las Victimas Dos de Mayo.** This park is very peaceful today, but it's had a surprisingly dramatic history. An arsenal was located here during the Spanish Civil War, where the courageous Madrileños came to collect arms in defense of their city (which was the last in Spain to fall to Franco's armies). It was also here that 43 Madrileños who had participated in the citywide uprising were brutally tortured and then shot by Napoleonic troops in the early hours of May 3, 1808. Their corpses were abandoned, but monks gathered the bodies as soon as it was safe to do so and buried them in the nearby cemetery of La Florida, now known as the 'Cemetery of the Victims of 2nd May'. You'll find it in the lower reaches of the park, downhill from the cable car station. Their common

'El Capricho' de Osuna

Madrid's most beautiful and romantic garden is lost in an urban wilderness of busy ring roads and neon-lit warehouses on the eastern fringes of the city. El Capricho de Osuna is a charming neoclassical palace built as a summer villa by the Duchess of Osuna in the 18th century, and is surrounded by glorious, extensive gardens. The formal French parterre leads into the English garden, scattered with charming follies, and a winding river leads to a delightful boating lake. The gardens are a trek from the city center (a 10-minute walk from the Canillejas metro stop at the end of Line 5 or a taxi-ride) but are worth traveling the distance. They are open at weekends only (until 6pm in winter and 9pm in summer) and admission is free. Picnics are not allowed, but if you're discreet and very careful about tidying up afterwards, it's unlikely that anyone will bother you.

grave is now marked with a marble monument, and a special service is held here every year on the anniversary of the uprising (May 2). If the cemetery is closed, you can still peek through the gates to admire a tiled reproduction of Goya's masterpiece depicting their execution.

⑥ Parque de la Tinaja.
Madrid's School of Ceramic Art (Escuela de Arte Ceramica) is located ithin the boundaries of the Parque del Oeste. Its grounds include the **Parque de la Tinaja,** an attractive, green expanse that sees surprisingly few visitors. The grounds are strewn, rather curiously, with antique train equipment donated by RENFE (Spain's national railway company) and are dominated by a huge, cone-shaped oven, originally built in the 19th century for the production of glass. *Metro: Ventura Rodríguez.*

⑦ ★ La Rosaleda de Madrid.
The undoubted jewel of the Parque del Oeste, La Rosaleda is a large and outstanding rose garden, scattered with cooling fountains and full of scented bowers and secret corners. It was first laid out in 1956, and annually hosts an important international competition featuring new

rose varieties. Most ordinary Madrileños prefer the more fun contest in which they get to vote for whichever bloom they consider the prettiest: people power meets flower power. *Paseo del Pintor Rosales.* ☎ *91-455-01-29. Open Nov–Mar daily 10am–8pm, Apr–Oct 9am–9pm. Metro: Ventura Rodríguez.*

⑧ Paseo del Pintor Rosales.
Running along the eastern edge of the park, the Paseo del Pintor Rosales is lined with terrace cafés and restaurants. It's always jam-packed late into the night in summer, when it's one of the few places in the city where a cooling breeze occasionally penetrates the heat. *Metro: Ventura Rodríguez.*

☕ El Molino de los Porches.
This restaurant has one of the most sought-after summer terraces in the city. Dine on traditional classics from grilled local vegetables to succulent roast lamb while enjoying scenic views over the Parque del Oeste and the Casa de Campo beyond. *Paseo del Pintor Rosales 1.* ☎ *91-548-13-36. Metro: Ventura Rodríguez. $$.*

Rose garden fountain.

Parque **del Retiro**

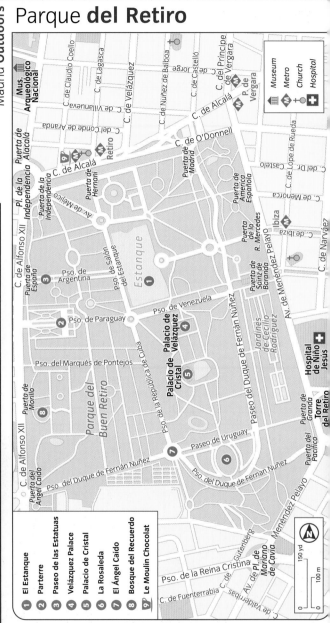

Museum 🏛
Metro ◈
Church ✛
Hospital ✚

1 El Estanque
2 Parterre
3 Paseo de las Estatuas
4 Velázquez Palace
5 Palacio de Cristal
6 La Rosaleda
7 El Ángel Caido
8 Bosque del Recuerdo
9 Le Moulin Chocolat

The splendid Parque del Retiro is one of the world's great city parks—as big as London's Hyde Park and as magical as New York's Central Park. These beautiful gardens are all that survive of the long-demolished baroque palace of the Buen Retiro, but are now every Madrileño's favorite weekend retreat. START: **Metro to Retiro.**

1 ★★★ kids **El Estanque.** The centerpiece of the park is this magnificent ornamental lake, dominated by the vast Monument to Alfonso XII, a 19th-century embellishment. The lavish royal barges that featured in elaborate court festivities in the 18th century have given way to bobbing rowboats and the flash of fat, golden koi carp chasing breadcrumbs.

2 Parterre. The *parterre*, now slightly dusty and neglected, is one of the few surviving corners of the original palace gardens. Formal and elegant with neatly trimmed low hedges, it is famous for an unusual cypress tree with thick, velvety clumps.

3 Paseo de las Estatuas. A sweeping promenade, flanked on either side by ranks of statues, this is officially called the Paseo de la Argentina del Retiro but more commonly known as the Paseo de las Estatuas ('Statue Promenade'). The

statues of every Spanish monarch were originally commissioned by Fernando VI to adorn the royal palace. Fortunately, he was talked out of this flamboyant but graceless gesture, and the redundant statues were relegated to various municipal parks around the city.

4 Velázquez Palace. This handsome pavilion of red brick, richly decorated with hand-painted tiles, was built in 1883 for a special exhibition. It was designed by Ricardo Velázquez Bosco and decorated by the ceramicist Daniel Zuloaga. It's now used by the Reina Sofía museum to host temporary exhibitions. *Paseo Duque de Fernan Núñez (Parque del Retiro).* ☎ *91-573-62-45. www.museoreinasofia.mcu.es. Free admission. May–Sept Mon, Wed–Sat 11am–8pm, Sun and public hols 11am–6pm; Oct–Apr Mon, Wed–Sat 10am–6pm, Sun and public hols 10am–4pm.*

Ornamental lake in Parque del Retiro.

5 ★★ **Palacio de Cristal.** One of the most striking buildings in Madrid, the fairytale Palacio de Cristal is a glassy pavilion overlooking a small lake. Another of the exhibition pavilions designed by Ricardo Velázquez Bosco in the 1880s, it is so delicately constructed that it almost appears to float. It's the perfect spot to spend an afternoon with a picnic and a book. *Paseo Duque de Fernan Núñez (Parque del Retiro).* ☎ *91-574-66-14. www.museoreinasofia.mcu.es. Free admission. May–Sept Mon, Wed–Sat 11am–8pm, Sun and public hols 11am–6pm; Oct–Apr Mon, Wed–Sat 10am–6pm, Sun and public hols 10am–4pm.*

6 ★ **La Rosaleda.** Come in May or June to experience these rose gardens at their finest. Laid out in 1915, the gardens are now one of the most tranquil corners in the Retiro. Tinkling fountains add a romantic touch.

7 **El Ángel Caído.** Madrid is proud to own what the city claims is the only statue of the devil in the world. The famous statue of the Fallen Angel sits at the southern end of the Retiro gardens, and depicts Lucifer's plummet from heaven as described by Milton in *Paradise Lost*. The statue was created by Ricardo Bellver in 1877, and subsequently acquired by the Spanish government.

8 ★ **Bosque del Recuerdo.** On March 11, 2004, 191 people were killed by terrorist bombs in Madrid. A fortnight later, a special agent was killed by a suicide bomb while attempting to arrest the terrorists. The 192 victims of the attacks are commemorated here in the Retiro Gardens by the Forest of Remembrance. Olive and cypress trees, one for each victim, have been planted in a special raised garden, which has been surrounded by a small stream, symbolizing life. Locals still bring flowers here, to commemorate their loved ones.

9 **Le Moulin Chocolat.** If you need a pick-me-up after a hard day's tramping through the Retiro park, wander over to this French-style *chocolatier* near the Retiro metro stop and pick up a fresh chocolate croissant or a cream-filled éclair. *C/ Alcalá 77.* ☎ *91-431-81-45. Metro: Retiro. $.* ●

Palacio de Cristal.

Dining Best Bets

Best for a Gourmet Blow-Out
★★★ Santceloni $$$$$ *Paseo de la Castellana 577 (p 108)*

Best Hip Café
★ Delic $$ *Plaza de la Paja s/n (p 104)*

Best Old-Fashioned Tapas
★ El Mollete $$ *C/ de la Bola 4 (p 104)*

Best Dining with Views
★★★ La Mirador del Museo $$$$ *Paseo del Prado 8 (p 106)*

Best Outdoor Dining
★★ Bokado $$$$ *Avda Juan de Herrera 2 (p 100)*

Best for Kids
★ Peggy Sue's American Diner $ *C/ Amaniel 20 (p 108)*

Best Chocolate con Churros
★★ Chocolateria San Ginés $ *Pasadizo de San Ginés 11 (p 104)*

Best Sheer Glamour
★★ La Terraza del Casino $$$$$ *C/ Alcalá 15 (p 107)*

Best Grandmother's Cooking
★★ Casa Alberto $$ *C/ Huertas 18 (p 102)*

Best Vegetarian
★ La Isla de Tesoro $$ *C/ Manuela Malasaña 3 (p 106)*

Best Lunchtime *Menú del día*
★ Al Norte $$$ *C/ San Nicolás 8 (p 100)*

Best Traditional Tiles
★ Cervecería Los Gatos $ *C/ Jesús 2 (p 103)*

Best Healthy Fast Food
★ Fast-Good $ *C/ Juan Bravo 3 (p 105)*

Chocolateria San Ginés.

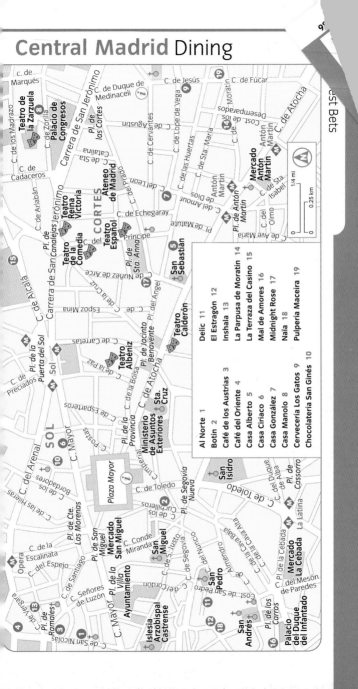

Al Norte 1
Botín 2
Café de los Austrias 3
Café del Oriente 4
Casa Alberto 5
Casa Ciriaco 6
Casa González 7
Casa Manolo 8
Cervecería Los Gatos 9
Chocolatería San Ginés 10
Delic 11
El Estragón 12
Inshala 13
La Parpusa de Moratín 14
La Terraza del Casino 15
Mal de Amores 16
Midnight Rose 17
Naïa 18
Pulpería Maceira 19

Madrid Dining

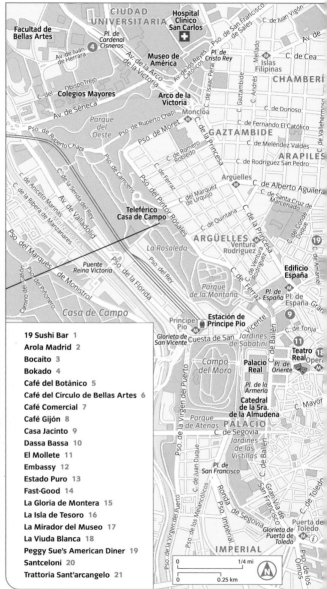

19 Sushi Bar 1
Arola Madrid 2
Bocaíto 3
Bokado 4
Café del Botánico 5
Café del Círculo de Bellas Artes 6
Café Comercial 7
Café Gijón 8
Casa Jacinto 9
Dassa Bassa 10
El Mollete 11
Embassy 12
Estado Puro 13
Fast-Good 14
La Gloria de Montera 15
La Isla de Tesoro 16
La Mirador del Museo 17
La Viuda Blanca 18
Peggy Sue's American Diner 19
Santceloni 20
Trattoria Sant'arcangelo 21

Information

Museum

Theater

Train Station

Metro

Madrid Dining **A to Z**

★ **19 Sushi Bar** CENTRAL MADRID *JAPANESE* If your taste buds are begging for a change from Spanish food, try this trendy, central sushi bar. Light and airy, with straightforward minimalist décor, it serves a wide range of Japanese cuisine, from tempura to sushi and sashimi. It also serves incredibly tender Kobe beef. Surprisingly creative fare, despite the very reasonable prices, includes a cocktail of sea anemone tempura with egg, or the tuna miso roll with asparagus. The set price lunch menus (12–20€) are excellent value. I like to drop in for a bite when shopping on the Gran Vía. *C/ Salud 19.* ☎ *91-524-05-71. Entrees 11–26€. MC, V. Lunch and dinner Sun–Fri, dinner Sat. Closed Aug. Metro: Gran Vía. Map p 98.*

★ **Al Norte** CENTRAL MADRID *NORTHERN SPANISH* The cuisine of northern Spain, which often features wonderfully fresh fish, is considered among the finest in the country. This chic restaurant, with its bold, minimalist furnishings, serves delicious dishes such as scallops with red grouper or lamb stuffed with prawns and pistachios. I often come to enjoy the excellent fixed price lunch (15€) out on the charming and compact terrace. *C/ San Nicolás 8.* ☎ *91-547-22-22. Entrees 14.50–20€. MC, V. Lunch and dinner Mon–Sat, lunch Sun. Metro: Ópera. Map p 97.*

★★ **Arola Madrid** CENTRAL MADRID *CONTEMPORARY SPANISH* Sergi Arola, one of the finest chefs in Spain, directs this upmarket restaurant located in the marvelous extension to the Reina Sofía museum. The huge, curving, deep red walls and ultra-modern décor are a fine backdrop to the impeccable contemporary cuisine. These are served as part of a fixed menu: the 'Pica-Pica' at 45€ and 'La Selección de Sergi' at 60€. Each comprises a selection of small dishes, which might include *fritura andaluza* (a platter of fried fish) or the *coca de cocochas de bacalao* (a kind of bread, topped with succulent cod cheeks). This is definitely a place to see and be seen, so come dressed to mingle with the fashionistas. *C/ Argumosa 43 (in the Reina Sofía museum).* ☎ *91-467-02-02. Menus at 45€ and 60€. AE, V. Lunch and dinner Tues–Sat, lunch Mon. Metro: Atocha. Map p 98.*

★ **Bocaito** CHUECA *TRADITIONAL SPANISH* This very popular, traditional eatery, with its colorful tiles and intricate wrought-iron decorative grilles, blends attractive Castilian and Andalucian décor. The menu is equally varied, with dishes from both central and southern Spain. The tapas are excellent, but you'll also find more substantial fare, including grilled meats, stews, fresh fish, and more. I particularly like the famous *mejimetas*—mussels topped with béchamel sauce and grilled until the crust bubbles. *C/ Libertad 6.* ☎ *91-532-12-19. Entrees 9.50–20€. AE, MC, V, DC. Lunch and dinner Mon–Fri, dinner Sat. Closed Aug. Metro: Chueca or Banco de España. Map p 98.*

★★ **Bokado** NORTHWEST MADRID *CONTEMPORARY SPANISH* The dynamic young Santamaría brothers are behind this trendy restaurant, wonderfully located in the Museo del Traje (Fashion Museum). The gleaming white interior is offset with elegant dark furnishings, but go for a table on the terrace, which overlooks the gardens and their delightful fountains. Try the hake with clams and Basque-style green sauce, served, like everything here, so beautifully it seems a shame to tuck in. In summer, you'll need to book a table well in advance. You can also try the exquisite *pintxos* (Basque-style tapas, made with slices of French bread with exotic toppings) in the adjoining café. *C/ Juan de Herrera 2 (in the Museo del Traje).* ☎ *91-549-00-41. Menus at 40€ and 45€. AE, MC, V. Lunch and dinner Tues–Sat, lunch Mon. Metro: Argüelles. Map p 98.*

★ **Botín** CENTRAL MADRID *TRADITIONAL SPANISH* The oldest restaurant in the world (founded in 1725), Botín is located in a cavernous cellar attached to the Plaza Mayor. It's firmly on the tourist trail, but even Madrileños recognize that the star dish—roast suckling pig (*cochinillo asado*)—is outstandingly good. *C/ Cuchilleros 17.* ☎ *91-366-42-17. Entrees 8.50–26.50€. AE, DC, MC, V. Lunch and dinner daily. Metro: La Latina or Ópera. Map p 97.*

Café del Círculo de Bellas Artes.

★★ **Café de los Austrias** CENTRAL MADRID *CAFÉ* An old-fashioned classic secreted away near the Royal Palace, where I like to while away an hour or two over morning coffee and the newspapers. The marble columns and worn gilt mirrors give the place plenty of battered charm, particularly in winter; in summer, pull up a chair on the small terrace. Simple tapas are offered, and there is also a *menú del día* served at weekday lunchtimes. *C/ Plaza de Ramales 1.* ☎ *91-559-84-36. AE, MC, V. Open 9am–midnight Sun–Thurs, 9am–2.30am Fri and Sat. Map p 97.*

★ kids **Café del Botánico** CENTRAL MADRID *TRADITIONAL CASTILIAN* Near the Botanic Gardens and the Prado, this charmingly old-fashioned café has a minuscule *comedor* (dining room) where you can tuck into traditional country dishes such as bean stew with chorizo, or *cocido* (the classic Madrileño stew). It has a great little terrace (although you'll be lucky to find a place). *C/ Ruiz de Alarcón 27.* ☎ *91-420-23-42. Entrees from 8€. AE, MC, V, DC. Open 9am–11pm daily. Metro: Banco de España. Map p 98.*

★★ kids **Café del Círculo de Bellas Artes** CENTRAL MADRID *CAFE* This elegant 1920s-style café is found in an Art Deco building, with swooping lines and huge picture windows. You can snack on simple sandwiches or tapas, or go for the well-priced lunchtime *menú del día*. I like to come here mid-afternoon, when you can often have the café all to yourself—sink into a sofa with a good book. A small admission fee is charged (1€) because this is a private arts foundation (see p 117, The Best Arts and Entertainment). *C/ Marqués de Casa Riera 2.* ☎ *91-360-54-00. AE, DC, MC., V. Mon–Thurs 8am–1am, Fri–Sat 9am–3am, Sun 9am–4am. Metro: Banco de España. Map p 98.*

★ **Café Comercial** CHUECA *CAFE*
This battered and old-fashioned café
opened in 1887, and the original
revolving door still functions perfectly. With its light-filled interior
scattered with marble-topped tables
and wooden chairs, it is imbued
with the patina of another era—
which even the rickety computers
offering erratic Internet access in
the corner can't dissipate. *Tertulias*
(the discussion groups that
Madrileños love) are often organized here. *C/ Glorieta de Bilbao 7.*
☎ *91-521-56-55. MC, V Mon–Thurs
7.30am–midnight, Fri–Sat 7.30am–
midnight, Sun 9am–midnight. Metro:
Banco de España. Map p 98.*

★ **Café Gijón** CENTRAL MADRID
CAFE   Founded in 1888, this was
once Madrid's most famous literary
café, frequented by novelists, poets,
philosophers, and thinkers. (Hemingway, who seemed to find a bar
stool almost everywhere else in the
city, turned his nose up at the Gijón,
which he considered 'full of show-
offs'.) Now, it's favored by smart,
older ladies from the Salamanca
neighborhood, besuited business-
men, and tourists in search of
vestiges of its romantic, literary

past. The artists have all gone, and
only a clock survives from the original 19th-century décor. Still, the red
velvet interior is a luxurious spot for
a mid-afternoon dose of coffee and
cake, served by long-aproned waiters. *C/ Paseo de Recoletos 21.*
☎ *91-521-54-25. MC, V. Daily
7am–3am. Metro: Banco de España
or Colón. Map p 98.*

★ kids **Café del Oriente** CEN-
TRAL MADRID *CAFE*   The huge terrace, overlooking the Plaza de
Oriente, offers some of the grandest
views in the city: the Royal Palace on
one side and the Teatro Real on the
other. It's best for tapas, snacks,
and ice creams, but you can also
enjoy more substantial (if rather
pricey) fare in the elegantly gilded
salons. *Plaza de Oriente.* ☎ *91-
548-46-20. Entrees 12.50–26€.
AE, DC, MC, V. Daily 8am–2am,
restaurant lunch and dinner daily.
Metro: Ópera. Map p 97.*

★★ **Casa Alberto** CENTRAL
MADRID *TRADITIONAL TAPAS*
With almost two centuries of his-
tory, the Casa Alberto remains a
stalwart of Madrid's culinary scene.
This is where locals come to relive

Churros con chocolate at Casa Manolo.

their grandmother's cooking with delicious, age-old recipes. Choose from classic tapas such as *croquetas* or meatballs (*albóndigas*) at the bar, or hearty stews and chops in the old-fashioned *comedor*. *C/ Huertas 18.* ☎ *91-429-93-56. Tapas from 3.50€, entrees 13.50–16.50€. AE, DC, MC, V. Tues–Sat midday–1am, Sun midday–4pm. Metro: Antón Martín Map p 97.*

★ **Casa Ciriaco** CENTRAL MADRID *TRADITIONAL SPANISH* A venerable institution, the Casa Ciriaco is one of the few surviving reminders of the Golden Age of the Madrileño tavern at the turn of the 20th century. Famous bullfighters, writers, and painters once made this their second home—when you've seen the beautifully tiled interior and met the courtly waiters, you might be tempted to do the same. This is the place to try all the Madrileño classics, from *callos* (tripe) to *cocido* (the classic pork stew, served only on Tuesdays), and the excellent *gallina en pepitoria* (a chicken casserole with garlic and saffron). *C/ Mayor 12.* ☎ *91-429-56-18. MC, V. Mon–Thurs 9am–midnight, Fri–Sat 9am–1am. Metro: Antón Martín. Map p 97.*

★ **Casa González** CENTRAL MADRID *TRADITIONAL TAPAS* A delightful neighborhood institution, Casa González has been going since 1931. It's a charming cross between an antiquated deli and a bar, and is the ideal place to try platters of pungent Spanish cheeses, hams, and cured meats accompanied by fine wines. If you like what you're sampling, the products can be purchased and vacuum-packed at the deli counter. *C/ León 12.* ☎ *91-429-56-18. MC, V. Mon–Thurs 9am–midnight, Fri–Sat 9am–1am. Metro: Antón Martín. Map p 97.*

★ **Casa Jacinto** CENTRAL MADRID *TRADITIONAL SPANISH* Hearty Castillian cuisine from the center of Spain is the draw at this welcoming tavern. The thoroughly *castizo* (genuine) decoration includes a huge bull's head and other bullfighting memorabilia. Good *callos* (tripe), a Madrileño staple, along with roast meats, are on the menu, as well as a small selection of seafood and salads. The lamb chops, *chuletas de lechal*, and the stews are especially good. *C/ Reloj 20.* ☎ *91-542-67-25. Entrees 10–19.50€. MC, V. Lunch and dinner Mon–Sat. Metro: Plaza España. Map p 98.*

★ **Casa Manolo** CENTRAL MADRID *TRADITIONAL TAPAS* Some of the finest *croquetas* in the city are to be found in this simple, archaic bar. It's located behind the parliament and in front of the Teatro de la Zarzuela, which creates an interesting crowd of politicians and performers. The wonderful little *empanadas* (small pies filled with meat or tuna) are also delicious. If you're near here at breakfast time, stop in for some *churros* con chocolate—fried dough strips dipped into a thick hot chocolate. *C/ Jovellanos 7.* ☎ *91-521-45-16. MC, V. Tues–Sat 9am–midnight, Mon 9am–5pm. Metro: Banco de España. Map p 97.*

★ **Cervecería Los Gatos** CENTRAL MADRID *TRADITIONAL TAPAS* The colorful old tiles, cheerfully random decoration (which includes basketball shirts and vintage posters), and welcoming crowd of locals make this an obligatory stop-off when exploring the Santa Ana neighborhood. The canapés (French bread topped with cured cheeses, hams, or smoked salmon) go well with the refreshing draught beers. *C/ Jesús 2.* ☎ *91-429-30-67. MC, V. Daily 11am–2am. Metro: Banco de España. Map p 97.*

★★ **kids** **Chocolatería San Ginés** CENTRAL MADRID *CAFÉ*
Possibly the most famous of Madrid's chocolaterías, with an enviable reputation for its *churros con chocolate*. Freshly prepared, and light as air, these long, deep-fried dough strips are utterly delicious. There are a couple of tables outside, or you can eat in the traditionally tiled interior. *C/ Pasadizo de San Ginés 5.* ☎ *91-365-65-46. No credit cards. Daily 9.30am–7am Metro: Ópera or Sol. Map p 97.*

★★ **Dassa Bassa** CENTRAL MADRID *CONTEMPORARY SPANISH*
Darío Barrio, a popular TV chef, is behind this fashionable restaurant, which is tucked away in a cellar. Palely decorated with austere minimalism, attention is focused firmly on the plate. The adventurous cuisine is based on the freshest produce, and the menu (which always features five starters, four meat dishes, and four fish dishes) changes regularly, reflecting what's in season. Expect the unexpected: a summer soup is served with slivers of cod and a ginger ale jelly, and the classic *rabo de toro* (oxtail stew) is

Daytime café Delic turns into a cocktail bar at night.

served with red wine and chocolate. *C/ Villalar 7.* ☎ *91-576-73-97. Entrees 20–42€. AE, DC, MC, V. Lunch and dinner Tues–Sat. Closed three weeks in Aug. Metro: Atocha. Map p 98.*

★ **kids** **Delic** CENTRAL MADRID *CAFÉ* By day a relaxed (if always packed) café, and by night a buzzy cocktail bar, Delic is the most stylish of the numerous cafés clustered around the lovely Plaza de la Paja. Snack on sandwiches, interesting salads, or tuck into cakes (the carrot cake is the best I've tasted in Spain). Kids can run around the square, while their footsore parents chill out on the large terrace. A gem. *Plaza de la Paja s/n.* ☎ *91-364-54-50. MC, V. Open Tues–Sat 11am–8pm, Sun 11am–midnight, Mon 8pm–2am. Metro: La Latina. Map p 97.*

★ **El Estragón** CENTRAL MADRID *VEGETARIAN* This attractive restaurant overlooks one of central Madrid's most charming squares (despite the current building works). The tables are scattered over three levels and the rustic décor is homely and friendly. The food is healthy and tasty, if perhaps slightly lacking in imagination, and the set-price lunch menu is a bargain at 10€. Curiously, coffee isn't served here, but there are countless cafés nearby to get a caffeine fix. *C/ Plaza de la Paja 21.* ☎ *91-365-89-82. Entrees 6–13.50€. AE, MC, V. Lunch and dinner daily. Metro: La Latina. Map p 97.*

★ **kids** **El Mollete** CENTRAL MADRID *MODERN SPANISH* A pleasantly dated tavern with rustic décor and just a handful of tables, El Mollete serves a surprisingly adventurous range of tapas and *raciones*. Along with homemade *croquetas* and *tortilla*, you might find caramelized *morcilla* (a kind of blood sausage) or duck magret with mandarin sauce. My favorite is the

Try El Mollete for an adventurous range of tapas.

classic *huevos estrellados*—a simple dish of potatoes and eggs that is somehow much more than the sum of its parts. They quite often have specials not on the menu—don't be afraid to ask the amiable owners for recommendations. Prices are extremely reasonable, and it fills up quickly with young regulars. *C/ de la Bola 4.* ☎ *91-547-78-20. Tapas from 2.50€. No credit cards. Metro: Ópera. Map p 98.*

★ **Embassy** CENTRAL MADRID *CAFÉ* Another of Madrid's classic traditional cafés, this is *the* place to come for afternoon tea. The range of teas and hot chocolates is served with cakes, elegant little sandwiches, and pastries. Join the immaculately coiffed Salamanca ladies and their miniature dogs out on the splendid summer terrace. *Paseo Castellana 12.* ☎ *91-435-94-80. AE, DC, MC, V. Daily 9am–2am. Metro: Serrano or Colón. Map p 98.*

★ **Estado Puro** CENTRAL MADRID *CONTEMPORARY TAPAS* One of

the newest tapas bars in town, this glittering fashion hot-spot is run by celebrity chef Paco Roncero (the chef from La Terraza del Casino). It's tucked away in a cellar under the NH Hotel Paseo del Prado, and is wildly decorated with tongue-in-cheek retro frescoes and thousands of traditional flamenco hair-combs set into the vaulted roof. There's also a terrace during the summer months. Traditional tapas such as *croquetas* and *callos* (tripe) are on the menu, but so are one or two more inventive creations such as the sublime deconstructed *Tortilla del siglo XXI* (21st-century omelet). *Plaza Cánovas del Castillo 4.* ☎ *91-573-95-54. AE, DC, MC, V. Lunch and dinner Tues–Sat, lunch Mon and Sun. Metro: Atocha. Map p 98.*

★ kids **Fast-Good** CENTRAL MADRID *CAFÉ* Celebrity chef Ferran Adriá led the boom in Spanish cuisine with his extraordinary creations at the legendary El Bullí restaurant in Catalonia. His latest project (in conjunction with NH Hotels) tackles fast food, and he has started a small chain of restaurants serving proper burgers, salads, and sandwiches, which are all prepared with flavorsome, healthy ingredients. In summer, they also serve artisanal ice creams, made exclusively from natural products. The brightly colored, modern surroundings make it a pleasurable dining experience. This branch is handy if you're visiting the Sorolla or Lazaro Galdiano museums. *C/ Juan Bravo 3.* ☎ *91-577-65-41. Burgers from 5.50€, sandwiches from 4.50€. AE, DC, MC, V. Daily midday–2am. Metro: Serrano or Colón. Map p 98.*

★★ kids **Inshala** CENTRAL MADRID *INTERNATIONAL* One of my favorite restaurants in the old heart of Madrid, this is a laidback and comfortable restaurant with North African décor (lamps, cushioned

The terrace restaurant at the Thyssen museum, La Mirador.

benches, tiled tables, screens). The menu offers an interesting mix of international cooking—Italian pasta, Mexican enchiladas, Japanese noodles, Moroccan couscous, and Mediterranean paella—although Spanish food predominates. The set-price lunch menu is a steal at 14€. *C/ Amnistia 10.* ☎ *91-548-26-32. Entrees 8.95–14.50€. MC, V. Lunch and dinner Mon–Sat. Metro: Ópera. Map p 97.*

★ kids **La Gloria de Montera**
CENTRAL MADRID *MODERN SPANISH* Part of a small chain, this offers style on a budget and a very reasonably priced menu featuring decent modern Mediterranean cuisine. Although you probably won't have your most memorable meal in Madrid here, it's relaxed, surprisingly stylish, and very comfortable. This makes it highly popular with young Madrileños and families who appreciate the low prices. But they don't accept reservations so get here early to ensure a table. Queues are inevitable at weekends. *C/ Caballero de Gracia 10.* ☎ *91-523-44-07. Entrees 5.95–8.95€. MC, V. Lunch and dinner Metro: Sol. Map p 98.*

★ kids **La Isla de Tesoro**
MALASAÑA *VEGAN* A charming vegan restaurant, with a dining room decorated like a beach bar in the Caribbean, this offers better and more imaginative food than most of Madrid's veggie restaurants. Each day, the menu offers the cuisine from a different country, so you might find a seitan couscous, Thai curry, or some wild mushroom pasta. Friendly and charming staff are the icing on the cake. *C/ Manuela Malasaña 3.* ☎ *91-593-14-40. Entrees 6.50–14€. Lunch and dinner daily. No credit card. Metro: Bilbao. Map p 98.*

★★★ **La Mirador del Museo**
CENTRAL MADRID *MODERN SPANISH* Many of Madrid's restaurants close down completely during August but this sublime terrace restaurant, on the roof of the Thyssen museum, is *only* open in July and August. The food—contemporary Mediterranean, beautifully prepared, presented, and served—can barely compete with the extraordinary views, which encompass most of the old city center. It's truly breathtaking. Book well in advance—this is the most sought-after terrace in Madrid. *Paseo del Prado 8.* ☎ *91-429-27-32. Entrees 12.50–26.50€. AE, MC, V Dinner Tues–Sun. Metro: Banco de España. Map p 98.*

★ **La Parpusa de Moratín** CENTRAL MADRID *TRADITIONAL SPANISH* This attractive restaurant, with exposed brick walls and wooden furnishings, serves delicious Castillian favorites at very reasonable prices. Start with the lettuce hearts served with pungent blue Cabrales cheese from Asturias, and then try one of the hearty stews. Service is friendly and efficient. It's handy if you are sightseeing around the Prado. *Plaza de la Paja 3.* ☎ *91-366-27-83. Entrees 8.50–12.50€. AE, MC, V. Lunch and dinner daily. Metro: Sol. Map p 97.*

★★★ La Terraza del Casino

CENTRAL MADRID *CONTEMPORARY SPANISH* A high-end restaurant in the historic casino, this is the most glamorous place to dine in Madrid. The gorgeous white décor is a 21st-century take on baroque opulence, with huge windows offering magnificent views. The award-winning chef, Paco Roncero, creates some of the most exciting contemporary cuisine in the city, with liberal use of foams and deconstructed dishes in the manner of his teacher, the legendary Ferran Adriá. Dress up, and prepare to have your tastebuds dazzled. *C/ Alcalá 15.* ☎ *91532-12-75. Entrees 39–68€. AE, MC, V. Lunch and dinner Mon–Fri, dinner Sat. Closed Aug. Metro: Sevilla. Map p 97.*

★ La Viuda Blanca CENTRAL

MADRID *MODERN SPANISH* A fashionable restaurant and lounge club on the equally fashionable Calle Campomanes, this is a fun place for a lively dinner. DJs keep the atmosphere upbeat, while diners tuck into carpaccios, salads, and creative versions of classics such as the chilled summer soup Salmorejo, or rice with wild mushrooms and langoustines. The adjoining club, La Viuda Negra, is a great place for an after-dinner cocktail. *C/ Campomanes 6.* ☎ *91-548-75-29. Entrees*
13.50–20€. MC, V. Lunch and dinner Mon–Sat. Metro: Santo Domingo. Map p 98.*

★ Mal de Amores CENTRAL

MADRID *MODERN SPANISH* For a romantic dinner, consider this appealing and cozy restaurant in one of the prettiest corners of old Madrid. There are two dining spaces: the candlelit cellar, with its ancient walls, is the most romantic. The menu features modern Spanish cuisine with international influences. The pasta dishes are generous and tasty, but you should leave room for the homemade desserts. *C/ Don Pedro 6.* ☎ *91-366-55-00. Entrees 12.50–22.50€. AE, MC, V. Lunch and dinner Tues–Sat, dinner Mon. Metro: La Latina. Map p 97.*

★ Midnight Rose CENTRAL

MADRID *FUSION CUISINE* The flashy bistro in the ultra-fashionable Me By Meliá hotel is one of the hottest dining places in town. The burnished gold and black designer décor provides a glitzy setting for the fashion pack, who come less to enjoy the original fusion cuisine than to see and be seen. Try the prawn and saffron croquettes or the grouper with artichoke ravioli. The kitchen is open until midnight, making it an excellent locale for late-

Midnight Rose bistro in the Me By Meliá hotel.

night dining. *Plaza de Santa Ana 14.* ☎ *91-701-60-20. Entrees 9–26€. AE, MC, V. Lunch and dinner daily. Metro: Sol. Map p 97.*

★ **Naïa** CENTRAL MADRID *MODERN SPANISH* A relaxed, modish restaurant on a buzzy square, this serves imaginative cuisine in sleek, New York-loft-style surroundings. Dine on specialties such as Santoña anchovies served with cherry and tomato *pisto*, or roast venison served with a celery and raspberry purée, while DJs spin ambient tunes. Finish up with the indulgent chocolate tart. There's a huge terrace out on the lovely square, and it's at the heart of one of the liveliest central nightlife zones. *Plaza de la Paja 3.* ☎ *91-366-27-83. Entrees 11–17.50€. AE, MC, V. Lunch and dinner daily. Metro: Sol. Map p 97.*

★ **kids Peggy Sue's American Diner** CENTRAL MADRID *NORTH AMERICAN* Children of all ages will love this shiny pink, 1950s-style diner. With its jukebox and chrome counter, it's a fun step back in time. The hot dogs, burgers, and milkshakes are all made on the spot in the open kitchen. The fries, prepared with the potato skins intact, are sinfully delicious. Make sure you book ahead, particularly at weekends, because it's very small and has just a handful of tables. There's another branch at Calle Eguilaz 1 (Metro: Glorieta de Bilbao). *C/ Amaniel 20.* ☎ *91-521-85-60. Entrees 4.45–5.95€. MC, V. Dinner Mon–Fri, lunch and dinner Sat–Sun. Metro: Noviciado. Map p 98.*

★ **Pulpería Maceira** CENTRAL MADRID *TRADITIONAL TAPAS* This appealingly ramshackle, traditional inn specializes in dishes from Galicia, in the northwest of Spain, which is celebrated for its seafood. The most typical Gallego dish is *pulpo* (octopus) served here in the classic style, with piquant tomato and paprika sauce. Other tasty treats include succulent mussels *marinera*, fish stews, and a small selection of meat dishes. At lunchtimes, they offer a *plato del día* for just 6€. There is a good range of regional wines—I love the Galician Albariño wines, which are the perfect accompaniment to seafood. *C/ Jesús 7.* ☎ *91-429-15-84. Tapas from 2.50€, raciones from 6.95€. AE, MC, V. Lunch and dinner Tues–Sat. Metro: Antón Martín. Map p 97.*

★★★ **Santceloni** CENTRAL MADRID *CONTEMPORARY SPANISH* Santi Santamaría is undoubtedly one of the finest chefs in Spain and, if you want a gastronomic treat you'll never forget, head to this elegant restaurant in the Hotel Hesperia. This Catalan maestro performs culinary magic, creating innovative dishes from wonderfully fresh seasonal produce. The menu changes regularly but might include such dishes as perfectly tender lamb with eggplant (aubergine), tomatoes, and olives, or roast partridge with thyme and black truffles. Every bite is a small slice of heaven. Push the boat out and go for the *menú gastronomico* (132€) or the *Gran Menú* (165€). *Paseo de la Castellana 577.* ☎ *91-210-88-40. Entrees 39–68€. AE, MC, V. Lunch and dinner Mon–Fri, dinner Sat. Closed Aug. Metro: Gregorio Marañón. Map p 98.*

★ **Trattoria Sant'arcangelo** CENTRAL MADRID *ITALIAN* This attractive, light-filled trattoria is a handy option if you're in the vicinity of the Prado. The lengthy menu includes all the Italian favorites from pasta to pizza as well as salads and carpaccios. It's a good place to bring children, with something to keep even the fussiest eaters happy. *C/ Moreto 15.* ☎ *91-369-10-93. Entrees 8.50–11.20€. MC, V. Lunch and dinner daily. Metro: Gran Via. Map p 98.* ●

Madrid Nightlife

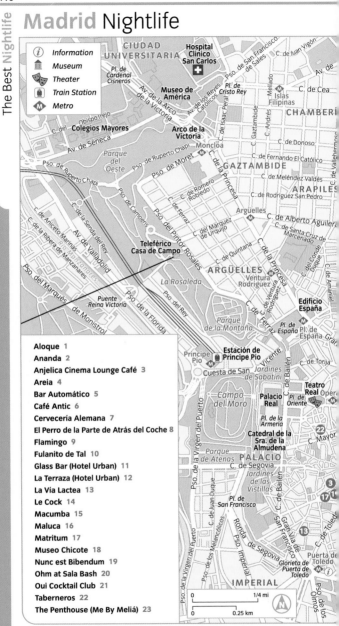

Aloque 1
Ananda 2
Anjelica Cinema Lounge Café 3
Areia 4
Bar Automático 5
Café Antic 6
Cervecería Alemana 7
El Perro de la Parte de Atrás del Coche 8
Flamingo 9
Fulanito de Tal 10
Glass Bar (Hotel Urban) 11
La Terraza (Hotel Urban) 12
La Vía Lactea 13
Le Cock 14
Macumba 15
Maluca 16
Matritum 17
Museo Chicote 18
Nunc est Bibendum 19
Ohm at Sala Bash 20
Oui Cocktail Club 21
Taberneros 22
The Penthouse (Me By Meliá) 23

Nightlife Best Bets

Best Old-World Atmosphere
★ Cerveceria Alemana, *Plaza Santa Ana 6 (p 113)*

Best Place to Meet the Next Pedro Almodóvar
★ Anjelica Cinema Lounge Café, *C/ Cava Baja 24 (p 113)*

Best Rooftop Views
★ La Terraza (Hotel Urban), *Carrera de San Jerónimo 34 (p 115)*

Best People-Watching
★ The Penthouse (Me By Meliá), *Plaza de Santa Ana 14 (p 116)*

Best Wine-Tasting
★★ Aloque, *C/ Torrecilla del Leal 20 (p 116)*

Best Classic Cocktails
★ Museo Chicote, *Gran Vía 12 (p 116)*

Best Oysters and Champagne
★★★ Glass Bar (Hotel Urban), *Carrera de San Jerónimo 34 (p 115)*

Best Cold Beer on a Hot Day
★★ Bar Automático, *C/ Argumosa 17 (p 113)*

Best Place to Chill Out
★ Areia, *C/ Hortaleza 92 (p 113)*

Best Nightclub Venue
★★ Macumba, *Plaza de la Estación de Chamartín s/n (p 114)*

Best Outdoor Dance Club
★★ Ananda, *Avda de la Ciudad de Barcelona s/n (p 114)*

Best Relic of the *Movida* Madrileña
★★★ La Vía Lactea, *C/ Velarde 19 (p 113)*

Best Weird Name
★★ El Perro de la Parte de Atrás del Coche ('The Dog from the Back Part of the Car'), *C/ Puebla 15 (p 114)*

Best Gay Party Night
★ Ohm at Sala Bash, *C/ Numància 179 (p 115)*

Best Disco Bar for Electropop
★ Oui Cocktail Club, *C/ Marqués Santa Ana 11 (p 114)*

Best 'After' Party
★ Space of Sound (Macumba), *C/ Plaza de la Estación de Chamartín s/n (p 114)*

Best Wine & Tapas
★ Taberneros, *C/ Santiago s/n (p 116)*

The Penthouse is a great place for people watching.

Madrid Nightlife A to Z

The century-old Cerveceria Alemana.

Bars & Pubs

★ **Anjelica Cinema Lounge Café** CENTRAL MADRID This relaxed, boho bar attached to a small art cinema serves tapas, snacks, and cocktails late into the night. Hang out with Madrid's young intellectuals, and join in with the organized talks and debates. *C/ Cava Baja 24.* 📞 *91-366-04-94. Tapas from 1.50€. Sun–Wed midday–1am, Thurs–Sat midday–2.30am. Metro: Latina. Map p 110.*

★ **Areia** CENTRAL MADRID Sink onto one of the low sofas piled high with cushions, and enjoy the soft lighting, silk drapes, and chilled-out electronica, lounge, and world music from guest DJs. On Saturday and Sunday afternoons, there's a fine brunch (12–5pm)—perfect for banishing hangovers. *C/ Hortaleza 92.* 📞 *91-310-03-07. Metro: Antón Martín. Map p 110.*

★ **Bar Automático** CENTRAL MADRID A laidback student favorite on the popular, bar-lined Calle Argumosa, this is the place to start the night. In summer, the party spreads outside along the entire street, which is lined with terraces. *C/ Argumosa 17.* 📞 *91-530-99-21. Metro: Atocha or Lavapies. Map p 110.*

★ **Cervecería Alemana** CENTRAL MADRID This century-old, wood-paneled tavern hasn't changed since Hemingway once propped up the bar. Brisk waiters in long white aprons bring you excellent beer accompanied by good tapas. It's touristy but there's a faithful local clientele too. *Plaza de Santa Ana 6.* 📞 *91-429-70-33. Metro: Sol. Map p 110.*

★ **La Vía Lactea** CENTRAL MADRID A veteran of the Madrileño Movida of the 1980s, this is one of the city's oldest haunts. A new generation of arty, alternative types hangs out under the vaulted ceilings, completely covered in old movie, theater, and concert posters. *C/ Velarde 19.* ☎ *91-446-75-81. Metro: Bilbao or Tribunal. Map p 110.*

★ **Le Cock** CENTRAL MADRID An upscale, tranquil bar where you can lounge on sofas and try a well-mixed cocktail. Comfortable without being stuffy, and popular without being too fashionable, it's deservedly one of the best-loved bars. During the early evenings, it's a great place to while away an hour or two. Later on and at weekends, the music and clientele liven up. *Cl de la Reina 16.* ☎ *91-532-28-26. Metro: Gran Vía or Sevilla. Map p 110.*

★ **Maluca** CENTRAL MADRID There aren't too many places in Madrid that will serve you a fresh strawberry daiquiri, but stylish Maluca always comes through. It's one of the smallest bars on this busy, bar-lined street, and it's one of my favorites for starting the long Madrid night. *C/ Calatrava 16.* ☎ *91-356-09-96. Metro: La Latina. Map p 110.*

Dance Clubs
★★ **Ananda** CENTRAL MADRID A car park near Atocha train station might not seem like the ideal venue for the city's biggest outdoor club, but one glimpse of Ananda's Asian-inspired décor will reassure demanding clubbers. Perhaps Madrid's most popular summer venue, its vast terrace with wicker loungers, Hindu sculptures, and lamps, packs out every weekend. *Avda de la Ciudad de Barcelona s/n.* ☎ *91-506-02-56. Metro: Atocha. Map p 110.*

★ **El Perro de la Parte de Atrás del Coche** CENTRAL MADRID Besides the weirdest of names ('The Dog from the Back Part of the Car'), this basement dive is one of the hippest club-cum-live music venues with a slick, alternative crowd. Eclectic sounds from soul and funk to electronica will

have you dancing until dawn. *C/ Puebla 15.* ☎ *91-521-03-25. Cover 8€, includes drink. Metro: Callao. Map p 110.*

★★ **Flamingo** CENTRAL MADRID A huge, emblematic club in the city center, the Sala Flamingo hosts three very popular club nights. Reggae rules on Thursdays with Island Sound System; on Friday, the young flock to Ocho y Medio; and on Saturdays indie fans and Goths gather for Deep Hole. *C/ Mesonero Romanos 13.* ☎ *91-541-35-00. Cover 6–10€, includes drink. Metro: Gran Vía. Map p 110.*

★★ **Macumba** NORTH MADRID Probably the best venue here, this huge club has the city's finest sound system and hosts several top club nights. Danzoo, on Saturday nights, attracts the best international DJs and is currently the best night in town. The Sunday morning 'after' party, Space of Sound, is legendary. *Plaza de la Estación de Chamartín s/n.* ☎ *91-506-02-56. Cover 10–20€ usually includes drink. Metro: Chamartín. Map p 110.*

★ **Oui Cocktail Club** CENTRAL MADRID This stylish disco-bar has bounced around the city in an effort

Glass Bar at Hotel Urban.

La Terraza at Hotel Urban.

to find a permanent home, but now it's clearly here to stay. Talented DJs keep the young, hip crowd going with the latest electropop. *C/ Marqués de Santa Ana 11.* ☎ *91-532-28-26. Usually no cover. Metro: Tribunal or Noviciado. Map p 110.*

Gay & Lesbian Bars/Clubs

Café Antic CENTRAL MADRID A classic in Chueca, the main gay neighborhood in central Madrid, this pretty cocktail bar, with its over-the-top baroque décor, hushed corners, and romantic candlelight, is perfect for romantic trysts or just a conversation. The clientele is largely, but not exclusively, gay. *Cl Hortaleza 4. no phone. No cover. Metro: Gran Vía. Map p 110.*

Fulanito de Tal CENTRAL MADRID One of the most popular lesbian venues in Chueca, this friendly disco-bar is on two levels and hosts everything from fashion shows to live music. Gays and straights are welcome, and it's popular with creative types. *C/ Conde de Xiquena 2.* ☎ *91-531-01-32. No cover. Metro: Chueca. Map p 110.*

★ **Ohm at Sala Bash** CENTRAL MADRID Sala Bash is a massive, mythical club in the city center. The biggest party is Ohm, on Fridays and Saturdays, which, although ostensibly gay, attracts a mixed crowd. Ohm was once legendary, but has gone off the boil in recent years. Even so, it still has no serious competition. *Plaza Callao 4.* ☎ *91-531-01-32. Cover 10–15€ includes drink. Metro: Callao. Map p 110.*

Lounges & Designer Cocktail Bars

★ **Glass Bar (Hotel Urban)** CENTRAL MADRID It doesn't get much cooler than this: the ultra-slick Hotel Urban's oyster bar is made entirely of glass, from the huge windows to the tables and chairs. Not the place for shrinking violets, this is all about looking good and being seen. Unpack those Manolos. *Carrera de San Jerónimo 34.* ☎ *91-787-77-70. Metro: Sevilla. Map p 110.*

★ **La Terraza (Hotel Urban)** CENTRAL MADRID The Hotel Urban's rooftop bar is the place to be once summer arrives. Sip a cocktail under the stars, as DJs spin mellow sounds. There are just as many people showing off up here as at the Glass Bar downstairs (see above), but the feel is more relaxed. *Carrera de San Jerónimo 34.* ☎ *91-787-77-70. Metro: Sevilla. Map p 110.*

★ **Museo Chicote** CENTRAL MADRID Countless icons of the 20th century, including Ava Gardner and Frank Sinatra, have passed through the doors of Chicote, Madrid's first and most celebrated cocktail club. Its elegantly preserved Art Deco décor makes it a special place for a drink. Different DJs every night crank up the chilled-out lounge music later on, when it fills with a younger crowd. *Gran Vía 12.* ☎ *91-532-67-37. Metro: Gran Vía. Map p 110.*

★ **The Penthouse (Me By Meliá)** CENTRAL MADRID Beloved by Madrileño fashionistas, the rooftop bar at the ultra-stylish Me By Meliá hotel is one of the city's favorite hangouts. Swoop up in the private lift to join the *gente guapa* (beautiful people) for cocktails, music, and incredible views over the old city. There's a great Sunday brunch, where you're bound to spot the odd celebrity. *Plaza de Santa Ana 14.* ☎ *91-701-60-00. Metro: Sol. Map p 110.*

Wine Bars

★ **Aloque** CENTRAL MADRID This tiny bar has a big reputation for its incredible selection of wines: there are more than 1,000 on the wine list. Unusually, it also offers a good choice of wines by the glass (these change regularly). Wine-tasting events and courses are also arranged. The tapas and *raciones* are excellent, and prices are extremely reasonable, so get here early to grab a table. *C/ Torrecilla del Leal 20.* ☎ *91-528-36-62. Metro: Lavapiés or Antón Martín. Map p 110.*

★ **Matritum** CENTRAL MADRID Small, stylish, and extremely popular, Matritum offers a wide and well-chosen wine selection accompanied by gourmet tapas. It's a good place to try wines from Spain's emerging boutique wineries. Staff are usually happy to give advice, but be here on the dot at 8.30pm if you want a seat. *C/ Cava Alta 16.* ☎ *91-528-36-62. Metro: Lavapiés or Antón Martín. Map p 110.*

★ **Nunc est Bibendum** CENTRAL MADRID You can't miss this tavern, which has a 'Michelin-Man' style cartoon splashed across the façade. Inside, it is spacious and stylish, with a semi-circular bar and a dining area with wooden tables and chairs. The wine list offers about 50 wines, mostly from the better-known Spanish bodegas, and the tapas are tasty and creative. It can be uncomfortably overcrowded, particularly in the post-Rastro mayhem on Sundays, so I prefer to come midweek. *C/ Cava Alta 13.* ☎ *91-366-52-10. Metro: La Latina. Map p 110.*

★★ **Taberneros** CENTRAL MADRID This attractive modern tavern is another reliable option for fine wines and excellent tapas. It's worth getting here early to ensure a table. An extensive wine list, knowledgeable staff who are happy to make recommendations, surprisingly creative food, and very reasonable prices make this a sound choice. *C/ Santiago 9.* ☎ *91-542-21-60. Metro: Ópera. Map p 110.* ●

Madrid Arts & Entertainment

Auditorio Nacional de Música 1
Café Central 2
Café Jazz Populart 3
Café La Palma 4
Cardamomo 5
Casa Patas 6
Cine Verdi 7
Clamores 8
Corral de la Morería 9
El Juglar 10
El Junco 11
Filmoteca (Ciné Doré) 12
La Boca del Lobo 13
Las Carboneras 14
Real Madrid –
  Estadio Santiago Bernabéu 15
Teatro Fernán Gómez 16
Teatro Real 17
Yelmo Cines Ideal 18

CIUDAD UNIVERSITARIA

Hospital Clínico San Carlos
Museo de América
Arco de la Victoria
Moncloa
Pl. de Cristo Rey
C. de San Francisco de Sales
C. de Juan Vigón
Av. de
Islas Filipinas
C. de Cea
CHAMBERÍ
C. de Donoso
C. de Fernando El Católico
GAZTAMBIDE
C. de Meléndez Valdés
ARAPILES
C. de Rodríguez San Pedro
Argüelles
C. de Alberto Aguilera
C. de Santa Cruz de Marcenado
ARGÜELLES
Ventura Rodríguez
Teleférico Casa de Campo
La Rosaleda
Edificio España
Parque de la Montaña
Pl. de España
Pl. de España Gran
Estación de Príncipe Pío
Príncipe Pío
Glorieta de San Vicente
Cuesta de San Jardines de Sabatini
C. de Torija
Casa de Campo
Lago Casa de Campo
Embarcadero
Lago
Puerta del Ángel
Puente del Rey
Campo del Moro
Palacio Real
Pl. de Oriente
Teatro Real
Opera
Pl. de la Armería
Catedral de la Sra. de la Almudena
C. Mayor
Puente de Segovia
Parque de Atenas
PALACIO
C. de Segovia
Jardines de las Vistillas
Puerta del Ángel
Avenida de Portugal
Paseo de Extremadura
PUERTA DEL ÁNGEL
Parque de Caramuel
Pl. de San Francisco
Ronda de Segovia
Gran Vía de San Francisco
Puerta de Toledo
Glorieta de Puerta de Toledo
IMPERIAL

(i) Information
🏛 Museum
🚉 Train Station
Ⓜ Metro

0   1/4 mi
0   0.25 km

Pso. de los. Pontones

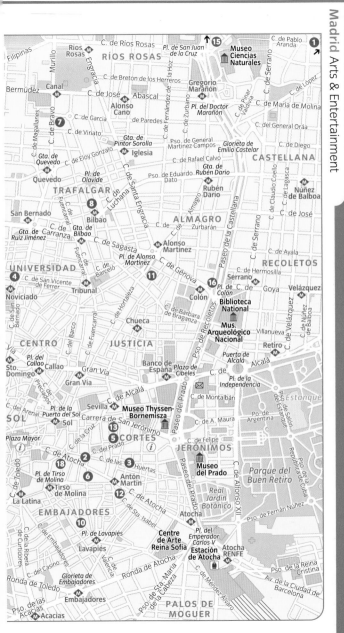

Arts & Entertainment Best Bets

Best **Concert Acoustics**
★★ Auditorio Nacional de Música, C/ Príncipe de Vergara 146 (p 121)

Best **Jazz Club for Romance**
★★ Café Central, Plaza del Ángel 10 (p 122)

Best **Basement Jazz Club**
★★ El Junco, Plaza de Santa Bárbara 10 (p 123)

Best **Flamenco, Flashy Dresses and All**
★★ Casa Patas, C/ Cañizares 10 (p 122)

Best **Opera House**
★★★ Teatro Real, Plaza Isabel II s/n (p 123)

Best **Summer Performing Arts Festival**
★★ Los Veranos de la Villa (p 123)

Best **Sporting Event**
★★ Real Madrid, Estadio Santiago Bernabéu, Paseo de la Castellana (p 124)

Best **Theater Performances**
★ Teatro Fernán Gómez, Plaza de Colón (p 124)

Best **Original Live Music Venue**
★★ El Juglar, C/ Lavapiés 37 (p 124)

Best **Hip Live Music Shows**
★ La Boca del Lobo, C/ Echegaray 11 (p 123)

Best for **Informal Flamenco**
★ Cardamomo, C/ Echegaray 15 (p 122)

Best **Art Nouveau Moviehouse**
★★★ Filmoteca (Ciné Doré), C/ Santa Isabel I 3 (p 121)

Best **Moviehouse for Subtitles**
★★ Cine Verdi, C/ Bravo Murillo 28 (p 121)

Best **Alternative Rock Festival**
Festimad (p 123)

Best Opera House: Teatro Real.

Arts & Entertainment **A to Z**

Classical Music & Concert Venues

★★★ **Auditorio Nacional de Música** OUTSKIRTS

Madrid's main classical music venue is awkwardly located on the outskirts of the city, but it is home to the National Orchestra of Spain and is the first port of call of all major international orchestras on tour. As well as classical music, it offers jazz, tango, flamenco, world music, and virtually every other genre imaginable. *C/ Príncipe de Vergara 146.* ☎ *91-337-01-41. Tickets 18–60€. www.auditorionacional.mcu.es. Metro: Cruz del Rayo or Prosperidad. Map p 118.*

★★★ **Teatro Real** CENTRAL MADRID

The magnificent opera house (see p 123) also presents classical music. It is home to the Orquesta Sinfónica de Madrid (Madrid Symphony Orchestra). *Plaza Isabel II s/n.* ☎ *91-516-06-60. Tickets 7.60–262€. www.teatro-real.com. Metro: Ópera. Map p 118.*

Film

★★ **Cine Verdi** NORTH MADRID

An outpost of the popular Barcelona art cinema, the Verdi has a good mixture of the cream of Hollywood movies, offbeat classics, world cinema, and interesting seasons. All films are shown undubbed and with Spanish subtitles. *C/ Bravo Murillo 28.* ☎ *91-447-39-30. Tickets 6.80€. www.cines-verdi.com. Metro: Antón Martín. Map p 118.*

★★★ **Filmoteca (Ciné Doré)** CENTRAL MADRID

This is a big favorite of mine. Spain's national movie theater is housed in its oldest cinema, the beautiful, Art Nouveau-style Ciné Doré (built 1922). Film sessions are incredibly cheap, and feature cult classics, retrospectives

Art Nouveau styled Ciné Doré.

of actors and directors, and special seasons. There's a decent café and bookshop too. *C/ Santa Isabel 3.* ☎ *91-369-11-25. www.mcu.es. Tickets 2.50€. Metro: Antón Martín. Map p 118.*

Yelmo Cines Ideal CENTRAL MADRID

The most central of the multiplexes, with nine screens showing undubbed movies in V.O. (*versión original*). This is where you'll find the latest blockbusters shown in their original language with Spanish subtitles. *C/ Dr Cortezo 36.* ☎ *91-436-25-18. Tickets 7.10€. Metro: Antón Martín. Map p 118.*

Flamenco

Las Carboneras CENTRAL MADRID

This popular *tablao* offers dinner and/or drinks with a flamenco show. The food is very ordinary, but the shows, performed by top artists, are enthralling. Interestingly, it also offers courses and lectures (in English and Spanish) on themes relating to flamenco. *C/ Plaza Conde de*

Advance Tickets & Listings

For the latest concert, theater, and event listings, pick up a copy of the weekly *Guía del Ocio*, a guide to all entertainment in Madrid. It's available at newsstands and written in Spanish, but it's pretty comprehensible even to non-Spanish speakers, with a small section in English at the back. You can also try *In Madrid*, a free English-language magazine found in cafés and bars, or look at www.tbsmagazine.com.

Advance tickets can be purchased at **El Corté Inglés** (several branches, including C/ Preciados 3, 902-40-02-22, www.elcorte ingles.es). Other ticket services include: **Tel-Entrada** (☎ 902-10-12-12, www.telentrada.com); **ServiCaixa** (☎ 902-33-22-11, www.servicaixa.com); and **Tick Tack Ticket** (☎ 902-15-00-25, www.ticktackticket.com).

Miranda 1. ☎ 91-542-86-77. *Shows at 10.30pm on Mon and Thurs–Sat; additional show at 8.30pm Fri and Sat. www.tablaolascarboneras.com. Metro: Ópera. Map p 118.*

★ **Cardamomo** CENTRAL MADRID Young locals and foreigners in pursuit of *duende* (emotion and authenticity in the arts) flock to this flamenco bar, where shows take place on the tiny stage nightly between Tuesday and Friday. It's the kind of place where someone might pick up a guitar as another begins the rhythmic clapping, and they suddenly burst into an impromptu performance. *C/ Echegaray 15. ☎ 91-369-05-57. www.cardamomo.net. Metro: Sevilla or Sol. Map p 118.*

★★ **Casa Patas** CENTRAL MADRID An old friend, a prestigious dancer with a long career, recommends this flamenco show above any others in the city. There is a restaurant attached, but the shows are performed in a

separate, intimate room where you can feel the sweat of the whirling dancers. *C/ Cañizares 10. ☎ 91-369-04-96. Metro: Antón Martín or Tirso de Molina. Map p 118.*

Corral de la Morería CENTRAL MADRID This advertises itself as 'the best flamenco *tablao* in the world'. It's certainly one of the oldest and most prestigious in Madrid, and it attracts some of the finest performers in the flamenco world today. *C/ Morería 17. ☎ 91-365-84-46. Metro: Ópera or Sol. Map p 118.*

Jazz & Cabaret
★★ **Café Central** CENTRAL MADRID I love this romantic, dimly lit jazz bar, which occupies a beautiful turn-of-the-20th-century former mirror shop, full of gleaming wood and burnished glass. The highly talented performers are drawn from the wide spectrum of jazz styles and there is a different group each week.

Café Central for quality jazz.

The venue is very small and fills up quickly, so get here early to bag a table. *Plaza del Ángel 10.* ☎ *91-369-41-43. www.cafecentralmadrid.com. Cover 9–12€. Metro: Sevilla or Sol. Map p 118.*

★ **Café Jazz Populart** CENTRAL MADRID   It's always a squeeze at this classic jazz club in the buzzy Santa Ana district, which attracts a young, bohemian crowd. There are usually two shows a night, at 11pm and then again at 12.30am, and the performers come from around the world. *C/ Huertas 29.* ☎ *91-429-84-07. www.salajuglar. com. Admission free. Metro: Antón Martín. Map p 118.*

★ **Clamores** CENTRAL MADRID This small and much-loved basement jazz venue stages all kinds of concerts, including pop, rock, and world music, but its roots are firmly set in jazz and blues. Like many of the city's best venues, it's part of the La Noche En Vivo group: check out their website to find out what's on when: www. lanocheenvivo.com. *C/ Alburquerque 14.* ☎ *91-445-79-38. www.sala clamores.com Cover varies, usually around 9€. Metro: Bilbao. Map p 118.*

★★ **El Junco** CENTRAL MADRID El Junco is a young whippersnapper by the standards of most of Madrid's jazz clubs, but it has already won a place in every jazz enthusiast's

Madrid's opulent opera house Teatro Real.

heart. It has all the right ingredients for a musical dive, with low red lights, exposed brick walls, and huge black-and-white murals. There are daily gigs, plus jam sessions on Sundays and Tuesdays. *Plaza de Santa Bárbara 10.* ☎ *91-319-20-81. www .eljunco.com. Cover 9–12€. Metro: Alonso Martínez. Map p 118.*

Opera
★★★ **Teatro Real** CENTRAL MADRID   Madrid's opulent opera house is considered one of the finest in the world. It opened in 1850 and is a heady whirl of marble

Madrid Music Festivals

Madrid hosts several popular music festivals throughout the summer. **Los Veranos de la Villa** (information from www. esmadrid.es) is one of the most prestigious, a summer-long festival of music, theater, circus, dance, and more. **Summercase** (www. summercase.com) is another 2-day festival featuring top acts such as PJ Harvey, Kaiser Chiefs, and Interpol. **Festimad** offers 48 hours of non-stop alternative music from the likes of Linkin Park and Metallica (**Metro: Casa del Reloj,** www.festimad.es).

Estadio Santiago Bernabéu.

and gilt. A performance here is an unforgettable event—and surprisingly affordable in comparison with other opera houses in Europe. *Plaza Isabel II s/n.* ☎ *91-516-06-60. Tickets 7.60–262€. www.teatro-real. com. Metro: Ópera. Map p 118.*

Pop & Rock
★ **La Boca del Lobo** CENTRAL MADRID   On busy, buzzy, bar-lined Calle Echegaray, this stands out for its original and wide-ranging program of events, including DJ sessions, film screenings, art exhibitions, and book signings. Live gigs can be anything from rock to cabaret. *C/ Echegaray 11.* ☎ *91-429-70-13. www.laboca dellobo.com. Admission varies free–10€. Metro: Sevilla. Map p 118.*

★ **Café La Palma** CENTRAL MADRID   This labyrinthine, student favorite is a café, bar, exhibition space, and live music venue in one. Early in the evening, it is mellow and great for a quiet drink, but things hot up as the evening progresses. There are live gigs by small bands from Thursday to Saturday. *C/ La Palma 62.* ☎ *91-522-50-31. Admission to concerts 6€. Metro: Noviciado. Map p 118.*

★ **El Juglar** CENTRAL MADRID   This is a great, multifunctional space in the heart of multicultural Lavapiés,

with a relaxed bar, live gigs by local artists (pop, rock, and a weekly flamenco night), and DJ sessions. *C/ Lavapiés 37.* ☎ *91-528-43-81. www.salajuglar.com. Admission usually 5€. Metro: La Latina. Map p 118.*

Spectator Sports
★★ **Real Madrid (Estadio Santiago Bernabéu)** CENTRAL MADRID   Madrid's immensely popular football, or soccer, team—perennially one of the best in Europe—plays at the Santiago Bernabéu stadium. Tickets for matches against arch-rivals FC Barcelona are hard to come by, but you can usually get hold of tickets for other matches. For information on the Real Madrid Museum, see p 47, Quirky Museums. *Estadio Santiago Bernabéu, Paseo de la Castellana.* ☎ *91-398-43-70 or* ☎ *902-30-17-09. www.realmadrid.es. Tickets start at 20€. Metro: Santiago Bernabéu. Map p 118.*

Theater
★ **Teatro Fernán Gómez (former Centro Cultural de la Villa)** CENTRAL MADRID   This multifunctional space has a wide-ranging program including theater and concerts in all musical genres. Drama predominates, however. *Plaza de Colón.* ☎ *91-575-60-80. Tickets 18–60€. Metro: Cruz del Rayo or Prosperidad. Map p 118.* ●

Lodging **Best Bets**

Best for **Afternoons in the Park**
★★ AC Palacio del Retiro $$$$
C/ Alfonso XII 14 (p 130)

Best for **Would-Be Aristocrats**
★★★ Ritz $$$$$ Plaza de la Lealtad 5 (p 140)

Best **Business Hotel**
★★ Hesperia Madrid $$$$ Paseo de la Castellana 57 (p 133)

Best **Eccentric Charm**
★★ Hostal Fonda Horizonte $$ C/ Atocha 28 (p 135)

Best **Cutting-Edge Design**
★★★ Hotel Silken Puerta América $$$$$ Avenida de América 41 (p 138)

Best for **Fashionistas**
★★★ Hotel Urban $$$$ Carrera de San Jerónimo 41 (p 138)

Room Mate Alicia.

Best for **Sheer Glamour**
★★★ Me by Meliá $$$$$ Plaza Santa Ana 14 (p 139)

Best **Old-City Location**
★★★ Hotel Plaza Mayor $$
C/ Atocha 3 (p 137)

Best **Shopaholics**
★ Adler $$$$$ C/ Velázquez 14 (p 130)

Best for **Spa Treatments**
★★ Hospes Madrid $$$$ Plaza de la Independencia 3 (p 133)

Best **Boutique Hotel**
★★★ Las Meninas $$$ C/ Campomanes 7 (p 139)

Best **Affordable Design**
★★ Room Mate Alicia $$$
C/ Prado 2 (p 140)

Best **City Views**
★★★ De Las Letras H & R $$$$
Gran Vía 11 (p 132); and ★ Vincci SoMa $$$ C/ Goya 79 (p 141)

Best for **Families**
★★ Los Jerónimos Aparthotel $$$
C/ Moreto 9 (p 139)

Best **Rooftop Pool**
★ Hotel Emperador $$$ Gran Vía 53 (p 136)

Best **Family-Run Hostel**
★★ Hostal Barrera $ C/ Atocha 95 (p 134)

Best **Luxe Hideaway**
★★ Casa de Madrid $$$$$ C/ Arrieta 2 (p 131)

Most **Palatial Hotel**
★★★ Westin Palace $$$$ Plaza de las Cortes 7 (p 142)

Best **Airport Hotel**
★★ Clement Barajas Hotel $$$
Avenida General 43 (p 132)

Old Madrid Lodging

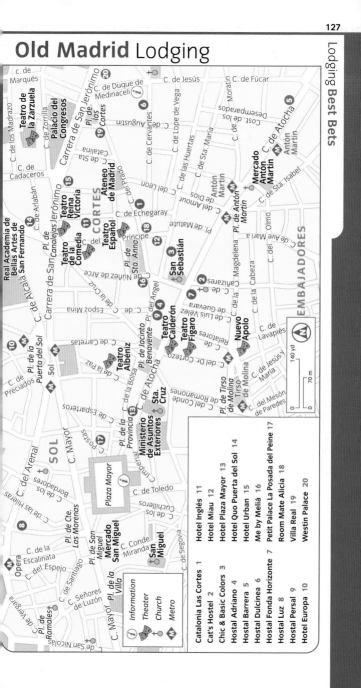

Catalonia Las Cortes 1
Cat's Hostel 2
Chic & Basic Colors 3
Hostal Adriano 4
Hostal Barrera 5
Hostal Dulcinea 6
Hostal Fonda Horizonte 7
Hostal Luz 8
Hostal Persal 9
Hotel Europa 10

Hotel Inglés 11
Hotel Miau 12
Hotel Plaza Mayor 13
Hotel Quo Puerta del Sol 14
Hotel Urban 15
Me by Meliá 16
Petit Palace La Posada del Peine 17
Room Mate Alicia 18
Villa Real 19
Westin Palace 20

Information
Theater
Church
Metro

Central Madrid Lodging

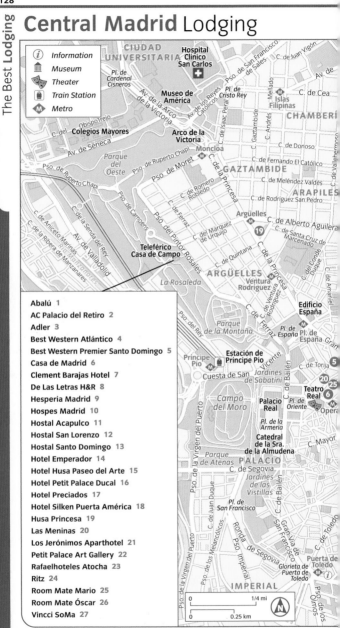

ⓘ Information
🏛 Museum
🎭 Theater
🚉 Train Station
Ⓜ Metro

Abalú 1
AC Palacio del Retiro 2
Adler 3
Best Western Atlántico 4
Best Western Premier Santo Domingo 5
Casa de Madrid 6
Clement Barajas Hotel 7
De Las Letras H&R 8
Hesperia Madrid 9
Hospes Madrid 10
Hostal Acapulco 11
Hostal San Lorenzo 12
Hostal Santo Domingo 13
Hotel Emperador 14
Hotel Husa Paseo del Arte 15
Hotel Petit Palace Ducal 16
Hotel Preciados 17
Hotel Silken Puerta América 18
Husa Princesa 19
Las Meninas 20
Los Jerónimos Aparthotel 21
Petit Palace Art Gallery 22
Rafaelhoteles Atocha 23
Ritz 24
Room Mate Mario 25
Room Mate Óscar 26
Vincci SoMa 27

Madrid Lodging **A to Z**

★ **Abalú** CENTRAL MADRID   A great option for fashion-conscious young couples, this offers stylish rooms and a friendly welcome in a spirited nightlife zone just off the central Gran Vía. The superior rooms are worth the extra because standard rooms are on the small side. Internet bargains make this a good deal. Bear in mind that the street is a bit run-down, and so be careful with bags at all times (as in any big city). And ongoing work within the hotel may result in unwelcome noise: enquire before booking. *C/ Pez 19.* ☎ *91-531-47-44. www.hotelabalu.com. 15 units. 75–350€. AE, MC, V. Metro: Noviciado. Map p 128.*

★★ kids **AC Palacio del Retiro** CENTRAL MADRID   With a privileged location overlooking the leafy Retiro Gardens and just a stone's throw from the Prado, the former owners of this elegant 20th-century palace used to exercise their horses on the roof. It has now been converted into a sleek, contemporary hotel and luxurious amenities include an enjoyable basement spa and smart restaurant. There's a babysitting service (with prior notice), and mums and dads will be grateful for the fabulous play areas of the Retiro Gardens across the street. Connecting rooms are available. *C/ Alfonso XII 14.* ☎ *91-523-74-60. www.ac-hoteles.com. 51 units. 236–464€. AE, DC, MC, V. Metro: Retiro. Map p 128.*

★ **Adler** CENTRAL MADRID   If stark minimalism is not for you, consider this classically elegant boutique hotel in the smart Salamanca neighborhood. The finest (and most expensive) shopping is on the doorstep, and the main sights of the historic center are a short metro journey away. As with most Madrid hotels, the expensive buffet breakfast is best swapped for a fresh coffee and pastry at one of the nearby cafés. Internet deals can reduce the room rate by more than half. *C/ Velázquez, 14.* ☎ *91-426-32-20. www.adlermadrid.com. 43 units. 473–665€. AE, DC, MC, V. Metro: Velázquez. Map p 128.*

★ **Best Western Atlántico** CENTRAL MADRID   A handsome

Roman Lounge, Casa de Madrid.

Chic & Basic Colors.

19th-century building right in the heart of the Gran Vía, this is a fantastic location. All the major sights are within walking distance, along with restaurants and shops. Rooms vary in size and comfort, but the nicest have balconies. There are inspiring views from the 9th-floor bar, which is also a quiet place to read and relax during the afternoons. *Gran Vía 38.* ☎ *91-522-64-80. www.bestwesternhotel atlantico.com. 109 units. 144–185€. AE, DC, MC, V. Metro: Gran Vía. Map p 128.*

★ **Best Western Premier Santo Domingo** CENTRAL MADRID   A great location just off the Gran Vía, an historic building, and an elegant interior all combine to make this a good, central choice. It's enjoyably old-fashioned, and the hallways are filled with antique paintings and sculptures. Ideal for a more mature clientele. *Plaza Santo Domingo 13.* ☎ *91-547-98-00. www.hotelsantodomingo.com. 119 units. 157–235€. AE, DC, MC, V. Metro: Santo Domingo. Map p 128.*

★★ **Casa de Madrid** CENTRAL MADRID   Imagine staying with a long-lost aristocratic cousin, in an 18th-century apartment filled with antiques and old paintings, and you

have an idea what this exclusive B&B feels like. Breakfast is served on silver trays, and drinks are provided from an honesty bar in the salon. Just a tiny sign above the bell denotes the entrance, and so consider using the chauffeur service from the airport (a fee is charged). *C/ Arrieta 2 (second floor).* ☎ *91-559-57-91. www.casa demadrid.com. 7 units. 256–417€. w/breakfast. AE, DC, MC, V. Metro: Ópera. Map p 128.*

★ kids **Catalonia Las Cortes** CENTRAL MADRID   An 18th-century *palacete* has been refurbished to contain this centrally located hotel. Two of the rooms (by far the nicest) still contain original frescoes, but the rest, though comfortable, are typical of chain hotels and rather anonymous. Take a look at the different rooms, if you can, before making a choice, and don't be afraid to ask to change. Handy for the Prado, and the nightlife of the Santa Ana neighborhood, it also offers excellent Internet deals, which regularly bring the price down to 99€. Triple rooms are available, as are babysitting services (on prior request). *C/ Prado 6* ☎ *91-389-60-51. www.hoteles-catalonia.com. 65 units. 99–385€. AE, DC, MC, V. Metro: Sevilla. Map p 127.*

Cat's Hostel CENTRAL MADRID

Backpackers love this basic hostel, which offers well-priced dorm accommodation, as well as double rooms with en suite bathrooms. The location is useful for Atocha train station and the three big art museums. The *hostal* is attractively set in an 18th-century *palacete*, with a tiled interior patio, and the party nights in the popular bar downstairs are always a big hit. If you plan on sleeping, bring earplugs. *C/ Cañizares (off Calle Atocha).* ☎ *91-523-81-27 www.catshostel.com. 15 units. 18–75€. Metro: Atocha. Map p 127.*

★★ Chic & Basic Colors

CENTRAL MADRID   Each room is individually and boldly decorated in a different color scheme at this stylish *hostal*, handily located near the Puerta del Sol. Rooms are small but unexpected extras include plasma TVs and a sitting room with basic kitchen facilities. If you prefer more space, consider one of the equally attractive self-catering apartments (in a different building on the same street). *C/ Huertas 14.* ☎ *91-429-69-35. www.chicandbasic.com. 10 units. 82–103€. MC, V. Metro: Sol. Map p 127.*

★★ Clement Barajas Hotel

CENTRAL MADRID   A great choice if you have an early or a late flight. It's a smart, modern hotel with neat rooms decorated in cool shades of cream and beige. It's located in a small suburb with plenty of cafés, shops, and restaurants if you choose not to eat in the hotel's own restaurant and brasserie. There's a regular 24-hour airport shuttle (5-minute journey), and bathrooms are stocked with lotions, potions, dressing gowns, and slippers, so you don't even have to unpack. The free WiFi and mini-bar are nice touches. *Avenida General 43.* ☎ *91-746-03-30. www.clementhoteles.com. 72 units. 110–220€. MC, V. Metro: Barajas, then shuttle. Map p 128.*

★★★ De Las Letras H&R CEN-

TRAL MADRID   A striking edifice from 1917, this has been sympathetically converted into a slick, welcoming hotel. Many original details, including the gorgeous tile-work, have been preserved, but plush 21st-century amenities including a wonderful roof terrace bar with knockout views, give it a contemporary feel. Each room is dedicated to a different writer, with quotations inscribed on the walls. I especially love the suites, which occupy the lofty cupolas. *Gran Vía 11.* ☎ *91-523-79-80. www.hoteldelas*

Clement Barajas Hotel.

Hospes Madrid.

letras.com. 103 units. 275–450€.
AE, DC, MC, V. Metro: Sevilla or Gran Vía. Map p 128.

★★ **Hesperia Madrid** CENTRAL
MADRID   A modern, sophisticated hotel, this is located in the business district in northern Madrid. It's a short metro ride to the sights, but you may not be able to tear yourself away from the hotel's outstanding (if small) Sky Gym, with state-of-the-art equipment and staggering city views. The Santceloni restaurant is superb (see p 108), service is excellent, and all rooms are soundproofed. An added bonus is the nearby shopping on Calle Serrano—the most glamorous street in Madrid. *Paseo Castellana 57.* ☎ *91-210-80-00. www. hesperia.com. 170 units. 176–363€. AE, DC, MC, V. Metro: Gregorio Marañón. Map p 128.*

★ **Hospes Madrid** CENTRAL
MADRID   A very pleasing fusion of classical architecture and chic interior design, this new hotel enjoys a perfect location at the entrance to the Retiro Gardens. The rooms are among the quietest in the city (definitely a bonus in Madrid), and are beautifully furnished with impressive bathrooms stuffed with prod-

ucts. The spa has a small pool and a host of luxurious treatments. Fashionistas will enjoy the chillout zone on the patio, and gourmets won't want to miss the excellent restaurant. *Plaza de la Independencia 3.* ☎ *91-432-29-11. www.hospes.es. 41 units. 245–720€. AE, DC, MC, V. Metro: Retiro. Map p 128.*

★ kids **Hostal Acapulco** CEN-
TRAL MADRID   Affordable, friendly, and central, the Hostal Acapulco has few frills but plenty of rustic charm. A tiny antique lift propels you up to

Hostal Acapulco.

Hostal Barrera.

the *hostal*, where chintz prints and dried flowers await. There are larger triple and quadruple rooms available, which are particularly good for families traveling on a budget. It's very centrally located, with all the main sights within walking distance. *C/ Salud 13 (4th floor), Plaza del Carmen.* ☎ *91-531-19-45. www.hostal acapulco.com. 16 units. 54–89€. MC, V. Metro: Gran Vía. Map p 128.*

★ kids **Hostal Adriano** CENTRAL MADRID   Bright, individually decorated rooms, a great location near the Puerta del Sol in the heart of the

Hostal Fonda Horizonte.

city, and rock-bottom prices make this a winner. Cheerful rooms are small, and bathrooms tiny, but all have air-conditioning, satellite TV with international channels, and free WiFi. If you don't mind a squeeze, some rooms can be adapted for four, making them suitable for budget-minded families. The frenetic nightlife of the Plaza Santa Ana is on the doorstep, so noise can be a problem (as it often is even in much smarter hotels too). *Plaza del Ángel 12.* ☎ *91-369-46-43. www. adrianohostall.com. 15 units. 65–95€. MC, V. Metro: Sol. Map p 127.*

★★★ kids **Hostal Barrera** CENTRAL MADRID   The simple little rooms—modestly furnished but all well-equipped with spotless bathrooms and air-conditioning—are perfectly adequate at this family-run *hostal*, but the real draw is the helpful management. Nothing is too much trouble, and they will even decorate your map with all the best places to see, eat, and drink. *C/ Atocha 95 (second floor).* ☎ *91-527-53-81. www.hostalbarrera.com. 14 units. 195–385€. AE, DC, MC, V. Metro: Antón Martín. Map p 127.*

★ **Hostal Dulcinea** CENTRAL MADRID   This is a good base for budget travelers who want Madrid's main sights on the doorstep but don't want to pay for extras. All the rooms are small and functionally furnished, but they are impeccably clean and some boast little balconies overlooking a quiet (for central Madrid) street. There are plenty of cafés close by for breakfast (I suggest walking up to the Plaza Santa Ana). *C/ Cervantes 19 (second floor).* ☎ *91-429-93-09. www.hostal dulcinea.com. 15 units. 36–65€. DC, MC, V. Metro: Antón Martín. Map p 127.*

★ **Hostal Fonda Horizonte** CENTRAL MADRID A small, family-run *hostal*, with an enthusiastic and multilingual young manager, this offers a handful of eccentrically, and occasionally, flamboyant rooms. The prettiest have flower-filled balconies overlooking the street. Not all boast en suite bathrooms, and noise can be a problem so bring earplugs. *C/ Atocha 28.* ☎ *91-369-09-96. www.hostalhorizonte.com. 65 units. 35–85€. Metro: Antón Martín. Map p 127.*

★ **Hostal Luz** CENTRAL MADRID For location, cleanliness, and rock-bottom prices, the Hostal Luz is hard to beat. Currently having a makeover, it's worth splashing out a few extra euros on the newer rooms in Hostal Luz 2, and return visitors will sigh with relief at the news that an elevator is being built. The bedrooms are filled with frilly curtains and bedspreads. There are no public spaces for dinner or breakfast, but you'll find plenty of cafés, bars, and shops close by. *C/ de las Fuentes 10.* ☎ *91-542-07-59. www.hostalluz. com. 12 units. 50–99€. Metro: Ópera. Map p 127.*

★★ kids **Hostal Persal** CENTRAL MADRID Overlooking a small, pedestrianized square linked to the bustling Plaza Santa Ana, this long-established *hostal* is a central bar-

Hostal Persal.

gain if you just want a cheap bed. Rooms (singles, doubles, triples, and quadruples) are plainly furnished and the décor is rather dated, but all have small en suite bathrooms, heating, and essential summer air-conditioning. There's a compact patio, and unexpected extras include free WiFi and discounts in the nearby Spa Excellence wellness center. Breakfast is included, but try to eat at one of the enticing nearby cafés. As in so many city center *hostales*, those ear plugs will come in handy. *Plaza del Ángel 12.* ☎ *91-369-46-43. www.hostal persal.com. 80 units. 65–110€. MC, V. Metro: Sol. Map p 127.*

★ **Hostal San Lorenzo** CENTRAL MADRID A rather plain hotel, just off the Gran Vía, it nonetheless offers reliably clean rooms with decent bathrooms, 24-hour reception, a breakfast buffet (for a small extra cost), and free Internet access. The rooms are furnished in pale, pastel prints and some have balconies overlooking the adjoining square. Noise can be a problem here. *C/ Clavel 8.* ☎ *91-521-30-57. www.hotel-sanlorenzo.com. 45 units. 60–102€. AE, DC, MC, V. Metro: Gran Vía. Map p 128.*

Roof-top pool at Hotel Emperador.

★★ Hostal Santo Domingo

CENTRAL MADRID   After a complete overhaul in 2007, this long-established hotel has emerged with a whole new 21st-century look. It's set in an old building, but don't be put off by the entrance and stairway, still in need of renovation. The rooms are compact but cheerfully decorated in bright, modern prints, prettily offset by original tiling and wrought-iron balconies. The bathrooms feature rain showers and even Jacuzzis in some rooms. Friendly, English-speaking staff are always on the spot to give recommendations. *C/ de las Fuentes 10.* ☎ *91-531-32-90. www.hostalsanto domingo.es. 185 units. 195–385€. AE, DC, MC, V. Metro: Callao. Map p 128.*

★ kids Hotel Emperador CEN-

TRAL MADRID   This large, modern hotel caters largely to business travelers, which can mean great bargains at weekends and during the summer (check on the Internet). Rooms are smallish and decked out in anonymous chain-hotel style, but they are spotless and well-equipped. Best of all is the rooftop pool, one of very few in the city, and the perfect place for a dip after a long day's sightseeing. The hotel is handily positioned on the Gran Vía, with plenty of shops and restaurants nearby, and most of the central sights are within walking distance. *Gran Vía 53.* ☎ *91-547-28-00. www. emperadorhotel.com. 232 units. 85–160€. MC, V. Metro: Santo Domingo. Map p 128.*

★ Hotel Europa CENTRAL MADRID

Established in 1917, this historic hotel is no longer the luxury retreat it was a century ago, but the traces of marble and sweeping staircase hint at its former glory. Now a modest hotel, it's unbeatably located overlooking the Puerta del Sol. The spick and span rooms are attractively, if impersonally, furnished, but all have modern bathrooms and some have small balconies looking out on the square. The doors are double-glazed, but light sleepers should still request an interior room. Friendly, English-speaking staff are great sources of local information. *C/ del Carmen 4.* ☎ *91-521-29-00. www.hoteleuropa. es. 99 units. 90–175€. AE, DC, MC, V. Metro: Sol. Map p 127.*

★ Hotel Husa Paseo del Arte

CENTRAL MADRID   Think location, location, location. Art fans will love this smart hotel, which sits next to the Reina Sofía contemporary art museum, and just a five-minute walk from the Thyssen and the Prado. Built in 2006, the rooms are crisp and modern, and some have floor-to-ceiling windows with breathtaking views. Great Internet deals regularly bring prices as low as 110€, which is good value. *C/ Atocha 123.* ☎ *91-298-48-00. www.hotelhusapaseodelarte.com 260 units. 110–160€. MC, V. Metro: Atocha. Map p 128.*

★ **Hotel Inglés** CENTRAL MADRID Established in 1886, this is one of Madrid's oldest hotels, which oozes creaky, old-fashioned charm. Rooms are functional and stuck in a 1960s time warp, but all are spotlessly clean and equipped with satellite TV and en suite bathrooms. The street is one of the busiest nightlife zones in the area, so come prepared for noise, or ask for an interior room. It is very central and makes a good base for sightseeing, particularly if you find one of the excellent deals on the Internet. *C/ Echegaray 8.* ☎ *91-787-77-70. www.hotel-ingles.net. 58 units. 120–130€. MC, V. Metro: Sol. Map p 127.*

★ **Hotel Miau** CENTRAL MADRID The Miau is nicely located overlooking the lively Plaza Santa Ana, in the heart of the busiest nightlife zone in the city. Interior rooms, without views, are quieter, but the best, in my book, are still those overlooking the colorful babble of the plaza. A very basic breakfast is included in the price. *C/ Principe 26.* ☎ *91-369-71-20. www.hotelmiau.com. 75 units. 195–315€. AE, DC, MC, V. Metro: Sol. Map p 127.*

★ **Hotel Petit Palace Ducal** CENTRAL MADRID Part of a fairly small chain, this modest hotel is situated in a converted 19th-century townhouse. It's just off the Gran Vía, with a wide variety of shopping and nightlife on the doorstep. Rooms, spread over six floors, are small but smartly finished with crisp, modern bedspreads and 21st-century amenities including WiFi and free Internet access. Go for the rooms on the upper floors, which are slightly quieter. Standard rates are high but Internet deals make it very affordable. *C/ Hortaleza 3.* ☎ *91-421-10-43. www.hthoteles.com. 60 units. 90–340€. AE, DC, MC, V. Metro: Gran Vía. Map p 128.*

★★★ **Hotel Plaza Mayor** CENTRAL MADRID The location of this family-run hotel, right at the entrance to the iconic Plaza Mayor, can't be bettered. One step from the hotel and you are in the historic heart of Habsburg Madrid. Rooms are modest but bright and welcoming, and staff are friendly and charming. The Palomar suite, a sunny attic room with its own tiny terrace boasting staggering views, is well worth the small extra cost. Book well in advance—this is one of the city's most popular budget hotels. *C/ Atocha 3.* ☎ *91-360-06-06. www.h-plazamayor.com. 34 units. 85–107€. MC, V. Metro: Sol. Map p 127.*

★★ **kids** **Hotel Preciados** CENTRAL MADRID This crisp, modern hotel is excellently located on the main pedestrianized shopping street, with all the main attractions nearby.

Hotel Miau.

Hotel Silken Puerta América.

Bedrooms are comfortable, and have been recently renovated (2008). Best of all, this is one place where street noise rarely penetrates, ensuring a good night's sleep! Staff are efficient and friendly, and thoughtful extras include chocolates on arrival and a free mini-bar. Suites are good value if traveling with children. *C/ Preciados 37.* ☎ *91-454-44-00. www.preciados hotel.com. 73 units. 160–290€. AE, DC, MC, V. Metro: Callao. Map p 128.*

★ **kids** **Hotel Quo Puerta del Sol** CENTRAL MADRID Smartly furnished in red, white, and black décor, this hotel has a great location in the heart of the city. Children are welcomed, and cots and babysitting services can be arranged. Superior rooms, with private terraces, are worth the extra. Internet deals regularly bring the price down to around 100€. *C/ Sevilla 4.* ☎ *91-532-90-49. www.quopuertadelsolhotel.com. 62 units. 150–290€. AE, DC, MC, V. Metro: Sol. Map p 127.*

★★ **Hotel Silken Puerta América** CENTRAL MADRID Wow! This isn't merely a hotel, it's an experience. A different, world-renowned architect has designed each floor in a stunning homage to contemporary design: crazy colors by Javier Mariscal, zen-like peace by Isozaki, and (my favorite) surreal

white sculptural surrounds by Zaha Hadid. It includes a gym and spa area, an astounding stainless steel pool, a garden, and an entire floor for business services. It is, however, located in a dull area on the edge of the city, en route to the airport, meaning a taxi-ride or metro into the center. *Avenida de América 41.* ☎ *91-744-54-00. www.hoteles-silken.com. 342 units. 450–4500€. AE, DC, MC, V. Metro: Cartagena or Avenida de América. Map p 128.*

★★★ **Hotel Urban** CENTRAL MADRID Fashionistas will be in their element here. The coolest hotel in town, it boasts glassy contemporary décor and every imaginable luxury amenity. It's one of very few hotels in the city with its own pool (tiny, admittedly, but still a boon during the searing summer heat) and the glamorous restaurant and rooftop bars are the refuge of the über-hip. It's full of fine art, including a small museum of ancient Egyptian antiquities. *Carrera de San Jerónimo 34.* ☎ *91-787-77-70. www.derbyhotels.com. 75 units. 195–385€. AE, DC, MC, V. Metro: Sevilla. Map p 127.*

★ **kids** **Husa Princesa** CENTRAL MADRID Large, comfortable, and convenient, this is well-located on a popular pedestrianized shopping street in the heart of the city, close to all the main sights. The impersonal décor, though trim and bright, reflects the hotel's ownership by a large chain and its orientation towards business travelers. But it offers excellent value for money if you can snag one of their regular Internet deals. The small gym with tiny indoor pool is a godsend during the summer. *C/ Princesa 40.* ☎ *91-542-21-00. www.hotel-husaprincesa.com. 257 units. 160–375€. AE, DC, MC, V. Metro: Sol. Map p 128.*

★★ **Las Meninas** CENTRAL MADRID   A perfect location close to the Royal Palace and the historic center, and elegant rooms coolly furnished in shades of cream and dove gray, make this an ideal mid-price option. Triple rooms are available for families and there are numerous restaurants, cafés, and bars in the vicinity. Thoughtful extras include DVD players and a small film library. *C/ Campomanes 7.* ☎ *91-541-28-05. www.hotelmeninas.es. 37 units. 109–195€. MC, V. Metro: Ópera. Map p 128.*

★★ kids **Los Jerónimos Aparthotel** CENTRAL MADRID When traveling with youngsters, I prefer to stay in accommodation with self-catering facilities. This aparthotel has simply furnished apartments (doubles, triples, and quadruples) that are cleaned daily, but the well-equipped kitchenettes allow you to throw together a meal if you want to stay in (although a café and restaurant are on site). Children love the small plunge pool and sun terrace. It's brilliantly situated behind the Prado, with the Retiro Gardens (acres of grass, play parks, and boating lake) nearby. *C/ Moreto 9.* ☎ *91-420-02-11. www.espahotel.es. 20 units. 120–240€. MC, V. Metro: Banco de España or Atocha. Map p 128.*

★★ **Me By Meliá** CENTRAL MADRID   The flashiest new luxury hotel in the city, this occupies a large wedding cake of a building constructed in the early 20th-century. Inside, dazzling white-and-gold décor is the theme, with models and DJs dangling languidly on huge sofas. Rooms are equipped with iPods and martini bars, and bathrooms come stocked with designer lotions. The Level floor boasts the most luxurious suites in Madrid, including a duplex in the uppermost

Reception, Hotel Urban.

Me By Meliá.

tower, offering panoramic views over the city. The rooftop bar is *the* place to be in summer. *Plaza Santa Ana 14.* ☎ *91-701-60-20. www.mebymelia.com. 192 units. 155–2255€. AE, DC, MC, V. Metro: Sol. Map p 127.*

★ kids **Petit Palace Art Gallery** CENTRAL MADRID   A chic boutique hotel in the smart Salamanca neighborhood, renowned for its plentiful shopping, this is full of contemporary art and stylish minimalist decor. Family rooms are available, with beds or fun bunk beds, and the diverting play parks of the Retiro Gardens are just two blocks away. There's also a sweet little garden terrace. *C/ Jorge Juan 17.* ☎ *91-435-54-11. www.hthotelesl.com. 61 units. 107–400€. AE, DC, MC, V. Metro: Serrano or Velázquez. Map p 128.*

★ **Petit Palace La Posada del Peine** CENTRAL MADRID   Occupying the building that contained the oldest inn in Madrid, this sits on a cobbled street right at the gateway to the magnificent Plaza Mayor. It has been revamped to house a modest, modern hotel, with chic, if rather small, rooms, and a smattering of original details to add coziness. All the main sights are just a short stroll away. *C/ Postas 17.* ☎ *91-523-81-51. www.hthoteles. com. 75 units. 190–215€. AE, DC, MC, V. Metro: Sol. Map p 127.*

★ **Rafaelhoteles Atocha** CENTRAL MADRID   This large chain hotel has bargain rooms and a good location close to three major art museums, Atocha train station, and the main southern bus station (good for late-night or early morning departures and arrivals). Internet deals regularly bring the price below 100€. Ask for one of the newly renovated rooms, which boast sleek modern furnishings in shades of cream and dark brown. It doesn't ooze personality, so is best for those looking for a well-priced, clean base. *C/ Méndez Álvaro 30.* ☎ *91-468-81-20. www. rafaelhoteles.com. 245 units. 99–328€ AE, DC, MC, V. Metro: Atocha. Map p 128.*

★★★ **Ritz** CENTRAL MADRID   The Grande Dame of Madrid's hotels, the Ritz is a huge, white Belle Époque-style confection wonderfully located right next to the Prado. Alfonso XIII ordered the original palace's conversion into a hotel, and it remains a favorite with visiting aristocrats (who usually choose the spectacular Royal Suite). Sumptuous, classical décor (no minimalism here), lavish amenities, and attentive service make this a very special place to stay. *Plaza de la Lealtad 5.* ☎ *91-420-37-67. www.ritzmadrid.com. 165 units. 510–4650€. AE, DC, MC, V. Metro: Banco de España. Map p 128.*

★★ **Room Mate Alicia** CENTRAL MADRID   Part of an innovative, small (but ever-expanding) chain, Alicia offers style on a budget in the atmospheric nightlife zone of Plaza Santa Ana. White predominates in the sleek decor, with splashes of bold color to add warmth. In summer, consider booking a superior room with private terrace, and take a siesta on the sun lounger. Hundreds of bars, restaurants, and tapas bars are right on the doorstep. Rooms are soundproofed, but invest in some ear plugs if you're a light sleeper. *C/ Prado 2.* ☎ *91-389-85-48. www.room-mate hotels.com. 34 units. 100–170€. AE, MC, V. Metro: Sol. Map p 127.*

★★ kids Room Mate Mario

CENTRAL MADRID   The original Room Mate hotel and still a big favorite of mine. This street is one of the nicest in the city, an elegant curve lined with leafy trees. Bold, contemporary décor, compact but well-equipped rooms, and friendly service are the hallmarks of the company. Staff are extremely obliging and extras such as free WiFi and a simple, free breakfast make it an attractive proposition. *C/ Campomanes 4.* ☎ *91-548-85-48. www. room-matehotels.com. 54 units. 85–160€. MC, V. Metro: Ópera. Map p 127.*

★★ kids Room Mate Óscar

CENTRAL MADRID   Another option from the excellent Room Mate stable. Although these hotels are largely patronized by young, cosmopolitan urbanites, the Óscar is a good choice for families with teenagers thanks to its great little rooftop pool area (but note that even guests need to book it in advance, and an extra fee is applicable except in the evenings). All the sights are within walking distance, and it's in the heart of the gay-friendly Chueca neighborhood, with its designer shops and bars. Breakfast is included. *Plaza Vázquez de Mella 12.* ☎ *91-701-11-73. www. room-matehotels.com. 75 units. 105–185€. AE, DC, MC, V. Metro: Chueca. Map p 128.*

★★ Villa Real CENTRAL MADRID

Refinement and luxury go hand in hand at this elegant *palacete*, which is located opposite the Spanish parliament and just a stone's throw from the Prado. The light-filled interiors meld classical elegance with contemporary art and furnishings, and there is an astounding collection of Roman mosaics and other antiquities. Not as cutting-edge as the Urban (nearby, and in the same chain), this nonetheless oozes effortless style. Summer rates, particularly in August, can be a bargain. *Plaza de las Cortes 10.* ☎ *91-420-37-67. www.derbyhoteles.com. 113 units. 171–436€. AE, DC, MC, V. Metro: Banco de España. Map p 127.*

★ kids Vincci SoMa CENTRAL

MADRID   Most Madrileño hotel rooms can be politely described as 'compact'. Here, however, most of the rooms are comparatively spacious, many offering wonderful terraces with room for sun loungers. Although not in the center, it is close

The Ritz.

to the Retiro Gardens and the upmarket Salamanca neighborhood; main sights are easily reached by metro. Drinks on the roof terrace offer unforgettable city views, and a good Mediterranean restaurant is on the ground floor. Triples and fully equipped apartments are also available, making this is a good choice for families. *C/ Goya 79.* ☎ *91-435-75-45. www.vinccihoteles.com. 61 units. 135–350€. AE, DC, MC, V. Metro: Goya. Map p 128.*

★★ kids **Westin Palace** CENTRAL MADRID   This Belle Époque hotel is a swanky Madrid institution, offering palatial luxury and stellar service. The hotel is currently undergoing restoration, so make sure you book a modernized room. The restaurant, though good, is rather overpriced; you'll find better, for less, in the neighborhood. The Prado is across the street, and all the main sights are within walking distance. Gym, hairdresser, and even a children's club (the Westin Kids Club) are among the hotel facilities. *Plaza de las Cortes 7.*

The Belle Époque Westin Palace.

☎ *91-360-80-00. www.westinpalace madrid.com. 468 units. 85–160€. MC, V. Metro: Banco de España. Map p 127.* ●

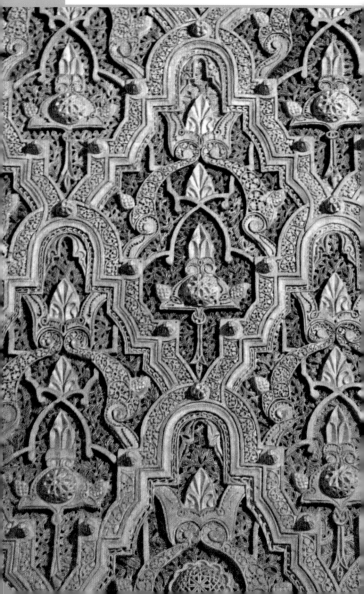

Aranjuez

1. Tren de la Fresa
2. Palacio Real de Aranjuez
3. Jardin del Parterre
4. Jardin de la Isla
5. Jardin del Príncipe
6. Museo de Falúas Reales
7. Casita del Labrador
8. Casco Antiguo
9. Casa Pablo

Information
Train Station
Bus Station

1/4 mi
0
0   0.25 km

Casita de Labradors 7

C. de las Moreras

C. de la Reina

C. Sóforas

Jardin del Príncipe 5

C. de Alvarez
C. de Quintos
C. de San Vicente

C. de Dr. Antaro de la Mata

C. Ciudad Social

C. del Primero de Mayo

C. de Lucas Jordan

C. de las Moreras

C. de Francisco Bayeu

C. de Almansa

C. de los
C. de San José
C. de las Flores

C. de Foso

C. de Abast

C. de la Primavera
C. de Alpajes

Av. del Príncipe
Av. de las Infantas
Av. de las Infantas

C. del Real
C. de San Antonio
C. de Gobernador
C. de Abastos

C. de San Pascual

Museo de Falúas Reales 6

Camino de colmenar

C. de la Reina

C. de Capt. A Gómez Castillón 9

C. de Stuart

8 CASCO ANTIGUO

Carretera de Madrid

Carretera de Madrid a Aranjuez

Jardin de la Isla 4

Jardin del Parterre 3

Jardin de Isabel II

C. de Gobernación

Antigua Carretera de Andalucia

C. de la Florida

Palacio Real de Aranjuez 2

Av. de Palacio

C. de la Florida

C. de San Antonio

C. de Abastos

C. Madrid

Pl. de Armas

Pl. de Parejas

C. de San Antonio

C. Palacio Silvela

Av. de Palacio

C. de J. Rodrigo

Aranjuez, beautifully set against the slow curves of the River Tajo, has been a royal retreat for several centuries. The Bourbons built the present, lavish 18th-century summer palace on the green riverbanks, and set it amid heavenly, tree-shaded gardens. The fine little town, which grew up around the court, is a delight to explore—a tranquil antidote to the energetic capital. START: **42-minute train journey from Madrid's Atocha Station.**

① ★★ kids **Tren de la Fresa.** Standard trains and buses regularly leave for Aranjuez, but nothing beats the romance of the Tren de la Fresa. In early summer, the 'Strawberry Train' puffs its way here, pulling a string of wooden carriages. Aranjuez is famous for its strawberries, and girls in medieval dress hand them out to train passengers. Harry Potter fans will feel like they're on the Hogwarts Express. 🕐 *1 hr. Reservations ☎ 902 24 02 02. Trains usually run weekends from early May to mid-July, but check timetables in advance at www.renfe.es, or at the tourist office. 25€ adults, 17€ children 4–12, free for under-4s. Prices include guided tour of the Palacio Real, bus tour, and admission to the Royal Barge Museum.*

② ★★ **Palacio Real de Aranjuez.** Felipe II commissioned the first permanent royal palace here on the banks of the river in 1561. It was subsequently transformed by the frivolous Spanish Bourbons, who sought to emulate the French court at Versailles. Most of what survives dates to the 18th and 19th centuries, and is as fluffy and ornate as the original palace was restrained and austere. Highlights of the rich interior include the rococo **Porcelain Room**, entirely covered in porcelain chinoiserie, and the **Arabic Cabinet**, which was inspired by the Alhambra in Granada. Anyone interested in royal fashion will be fascinated by the exhibition of wedding gowns worn by the present Queen, her daughters, and her

Palacio Real de Aranjuez.

Statue and fountain in the garden of the royal palace.

popular daughter-in-law Leticia.
🕐 *1 hr 30 min. Plaza de Parejas.*
📞 *91-891-03-05. www.patrimonio nacional.es. Oct–Mar 10am–5.15pm, Apr–Sept 10am–6.15pm. 5€ adults with guided visit, 4.50€ adults non-guided visit, 4€ children 5–16, free for under-5s. Palace plus guided visit to private salons 7€ adults, 5€ children 5–16, free for under-5s. Combined ticket to palace and Royal Barge Museum 8€ adults, 7€ children 5-16, free for under-5s.*

❸ ★ **Jardín del Parterre.** The palace is merely the warm-up to the gardens, which are the real draw of verdant Aranjuez. The formal Parterre gardens flank the eastern façade of the palace and are gracefully laid out in the French style fashionable in the 17th century. 🕐 *20 min. Oct–Mar daily 8am–6.30pm, Apr–Sept daily 8am–8.30pm.*

❹ ★ **Jardín de la Isla.** These charming gardens, just off the Parterre, are surrounded by the slow undulations of the River Tajo.

They are one of the few survivors of the old manor house that once stood here, which was used by Ferdinand and Isabella as their summer retreat before the construction of the Royal Palace. There are several beautiful fountains, all with classical themes, from a seductive Venus to a jolly Bacchus. 🕐 *20 min. Oct–Mar daily 8am–6.30pm, Apr–Sept daily 8am–8.30pm.*

❺ **Jardín del Príncipe.** This green, tree-shaded oasis is the largest of the royal gardens at Aranjuez and a sheer delight to explore on foot. It was commissioned by the future Carlos IV, then the Prince of Asturias (hence the name, 'the Prince's Garden'), and designed between 1772 and 1804. Huge trees—including oaks, cypresses, and magnolias—are elegantly and seemingly carelessly arranged around cool walkways. Fountains and statues are dotted in shady bowers, where smart peacocks strut and shriek. 🕐 *1 hr. Open Oct–Mar daily 8am–6.30pm, Apr–Sept daily 8am–8.30pm.*

⑥ Museo de Falúas Reales.

Languid royals once drifted along the river in their grand pleasure boats and barges, and these have been gathered together in the fascinating Museo de Falúas (Royal Barge Museum). My favorite is a lovely 17th-century Venetian gondola with gilded nymphs and flowers. ⏱ *45 min. Cl de la Reina, in the Jardín del Principe.* ☎ *91-891-03-05. Apr–Sept Tues–Sun and public hols 10am–6.15pm, Oct–Mar 10am–5.15pm. Admission 3€ adults, 2€ children 5–16 and seniors, free for under-5s. Combined ticket to palace and Royal Barge Museum 8€ adults, 7€ children 5–16, free for under-5s. Free on Wed for EU-citizens with photo ID.*

⑦ Casita del Labrador.

The 'Laborer's Cottage' was constructed between 1791 and 1803. Despite the name, it bears no resemblance to a cottage, and its function was entirely related to the pursuit of pleasure. A large, elegant summer pavilion, it is filled with an array of porcelain, statues, paintings, tapestries, clocks, and other works of art, all of which are painstakingly (and somewhat boringly) described on the (obligatory) guided tour. ⏱ *45 min. Plaza de Parejas.* ☎ *91-891-03-05. www.patrimonionacional.es. Oct–Mar Tues–Sun 10am–5pm, Apr–Sept 10am–6pm. 5€ adults with obligatory guided visit, 4€ children 5–16, free for under-5s. Palace plus guided visit to private salons 7€ adults, 5€ children 5–16, free for under-5s.*

⑧ ★ Casco Antiguo.

The elegant Casco Antiguo (old quarter) of Aranjuez is characterized by broad boulevards and expansive squares. Unlike other towns, which grew up organically over the centuries, Aranjuez was carefully planned and laid out in the 1740s. Numerous royal residences and baroque churches are incorporated into the fine ensemble. ⏱ *45 min.*

⑨ Casa Pablo.

A handsome, old-fashioned tavern established in 1941, this serves classic Castilian cuisine, as well as the sweet strawberries and plump white asparagus for which the town is famous. *C/ Almibar 42.* ☎ *91-892-11-48. $.*

Practical Matters: Aranjuez

The wonderful Tren de la Fresa (see p 145) is the most romantic way to reach Aranjuez, but only runs for a few weekends in early summer. Trains from Madrid's Atocha station (taking 42 mins, 3.90€ one way) are the most convenient way to reach the town. A bus service operated by Continental, ☎ 902-33-04-00, departs from the Méndez Álvaro bus station (1 hr, 4.25€). The **Tourist Information Office** is on Plaza de San Antonio 9, ☎ 91-891-04-27, www.aranjuez.es.

El Escorial

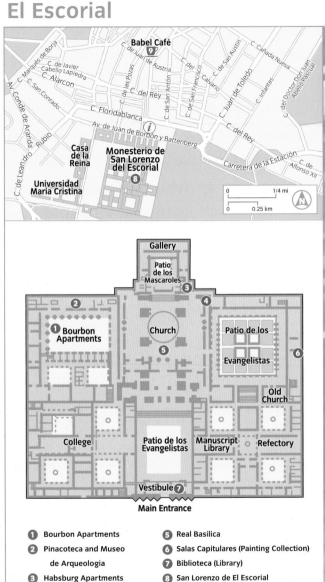

1. Bourbon Apartments
2. Pinacoteca and Museo de Arqueologia
3. Habsburg Apartments
4. Panteón de los Reyes
5. Real Basilica
6. Salas Capitulares (Painting Collection)
7. Biblioteca (Library)
8. San Lorenzo de El Escorial
9. Babel Café

Rising austerely from the Sierras north of Madrid, the vast Royal Palace and Monastery of El Escorial was constructed in the late 16th century for King Felipe II (1527–98). Built on a truly colossal scale, the palace-monastery also included a convent, school, library, and a royal pantheon: Spanish monarchs are still laid to rest here. It was from this mountain stronghold that the fanatically religious king ruled his vast empire, zealously stamping out all forms of heresy.

START: **One hour train journey from Madrid's Atocha Station.**

1 ★★ **Bourbon Apartments.** The fun-loving Bourbons disliked gloomy El Escorial, but they did their best to brighten up some of the apartments for their own use. Hung with fetching tapestries, they are the easily the cheeriest section of the palace. Their apartments also contain the **Sala de las Batallas**, a vaulted hall with an enormous fresco depicting great Spanish military victories. ⏱ *30 min.*

2 ★ **Pinacoteca and Museo de Arqueologia.** Galleries adjoining the Habsburg apartments contain two museums, which were added: the **Pinacoteca**, with a fine painting collection (including works by Bosch, who was much liked by Felipe II), and the **Archaeology**
Museum, with a fascinating exhibition describing the mechanics of the palace's construction. ⏱ *40 min.*

3 ★ **Habsburg Apartments.** The Habsburg Apartments are those created for Felipe II. They are surprisingly humble and delightfully intimate, with their alluring blue-and-white tiles and beautiful views over forests and mountains. In these charming rooms, Felipe II and his advisors heard the crushing news of the failure of the Spanish Armada and of the country's bankruptcy as Felipe II pursued his punishing wars against the Protestant Dutch and the Moslem Ottomans. It's a chilling thought. Felipe's apartments were built above the Basilica, and his deathbed is still pressed up against

The Royal Palace and Monastery at El Escorial.

Statue on the monastery wall.

the opening through which he could hear mass being said. 🕐 *30 min.*

4 ★ **Panteón de los Reyes.** When Felipe II conceived his new palace-monastery, he sought to find a suitable burial place for his parents, Charles V (Carlos I of Spain) and Isabella of Portugal. The spectacular, marble-and-gold **Pantheon of the Kings** contains 26 marble sepulchers, which contain the remains of almost every Spanish monarch from the 16th century onwards. According to an old tradition, queens are only interred here if they are the mother of kings. Queens who didn't bear a king, princes, and princesses are buried in the adjoining, labyrinthine 19th-century **Pantheon of the Princes**, added at the command of Isabel II. In a rather gruesome ritual, the remains of dead monarchs are left in the *pudridero* (Rotting Room) for 50 years before being moved into the Pantheon. The parents of the present king, Juan Carlos I, are in the *pudridero*, awaiting removal to the last empty marble sepulcher, and a decision has yet to be made as to

where the currently living members of the Royal Family will be interred after their demise. 🕐 *30 min.*

5 ★ **Real Basílica.** The Royal Basilica was the very soul of the El Escorial complex. It was designed, like the rest of the palace, by Juan Bautista de Toledo and his pupil Juan de Herrera, who was clearly influenced by that other great monument to the Counter-Reformation: St Peter's Basilica, in Rome. The huge, soaring dome, which echoes that of St Peter's, is all the more impressive for being virtually unadorned. The high altar, however, is a dazzling swirl of color and gold. The lavish altarpiece is flanked by life-size gilded bronze statues depicting Charles V (Carlos I of Spain), Felipe II, and their families. There are 43 altars, so that several masses could be said simultaneously. Some contain part of Felipe II's enormous collection of reliquaries, to which the king was very attached. More than 7,500 elaborate coffers allegedly containing the bones, hair, and nails of the saints are scattered throughout the complex. 🕐 *30 min.*

6 ★ Salas Capitulares (Painting Collection). The Sacristy and Chapterhouses contain more of El Escorial's vast collection of paintings, most with a religious theme, which are gathered beneath elaborately frescoed ceilings. The best, however, was creamed off for inclusion in the Pinacoteca (see above). ⏱ **20 min.**

7 ★ Biblioteca (Library). The beautiful library boasts gleaming wood paneling and elaborate frescoes. It was built to house Felipe II's enormous book collection, which numbered more than 40,000 volumes. Ironically, despite Felipe's avid support of the Inquisition that destroyed countless 'heretical' works, his library, watched over by Benito Arias Montano, contains priceless Greek, Latin, Hebrew, and Arabic manuscripts which were rescued from the flames. ⏱ **20 min.**

8 San Lorenzo de El Escorial. The sheer scale of El Escorial is overwhelming, but the relaxed little town of San Lorenzo de El Escorial, with its mountainous backdrop, is a fine place to recover. The *casco histórico* (old quarter) is appealing, with its arcaded streets and charming squares. A couple of outdoor cafés spread their tables onto the handsome Plaza de la Constitución—perfect for soaking up the sun after the chilly gloom of the great palace-monastery. ⏱ **30 min.**

9 Babel Café. A friendly, bohemian café, this is a great place to cheer yourself up after the gloomy palace. Live music and a lovely if small summer terrace. *C/ San Juan de Austria 7.* ☎ *91-896-05-22. $.*

Practical Matters: San Lorenzo de El Escorial

Trains (1 hr 5 mins; ☎ 902-24-02-02; www.renfe.es) make frequent departures from Madrid's Atocha station to San Lorenzo de El Escorial, but you will have to take a local bus from the station into the town center. Buses (nos 661 or 664) depart from the Intercambiador de Montcloa in Madrid, and arrive at the bus station on the edge of town. By car, take the A6 highway (toll) or the M505 from Madrid. The **Tourist Information Office** (☎ 91-890-03-13; www.sanlorenzoturismo.com) is at C/ Grimaldi, 4.

Royal Palace and Monastery of El Escorial: C/ Juan de Borbón y Battemberg s/n. ☎ 91-890-59-02. www.patrimonionacional.es. Open: Oct–Mar Tues–Sun 10am–5pm, Apr–Sept Tues–Sun 10am–6pm. Admission: 10€ adults with guided visit, 8€ adults for self-guided visit. 3.5–4€ senior citizens and children aged 5–16. Under 5s free. Free admission to Basilica only.

Toledo

1. Museo de Santa Cruz
2. Alcázar
3. Cathedral
4. Iglesia de Sant Tomé
5. Casa-Museo El Greco
6. Sinagoga del Tránsito
   and Museo Sefardi
7. Sinagoga de Santa Maria
   la Blanca
8. Monasterio de San Juan
   de los Reyes

Toledo is a captivating city, coiled sinuously around a hilltop overlooking the River Tajo. El Greco, who lived here for decades, never tired of painting its elegant silhouette. The most striking monument is the huge cathedral, but mosques and synagogues attest to Toledo's historic reputation for religious tolerance.
START: **30-minute train journey from Madrid's Atocha Station.**

1 ★ Museo de Santa Cruz.
The majestic Renaissance Hospital de Santa Cruz is adorned with intricate Plateresque stonework. Now an excellent museum with collections spanning everything from painting to archaeology, it is linked to the Prado and often presents excellent temporary exhibitions. ⏱ *30 min. C/ Cervantes 3.* ☎ *952-22-10-36. Admission free. Mon–Sat 10am–6.30pm and Sun 10am–2pm.*

2 ★ Alcázar. This huge 16th-century fortress with its spiky towers has functioned for many years as an army museum, and, controversially, as one of very few places left in Spain where Franco's memory was preserved with any affection. The fortress is currently undergoing major refurbishment and is slated to re-open in 2009 (confirm with the

The 16th-century Alcázar.

tourist office). *Cuesta de Carlos V.* ☎ *925-22-16-73.*

3 ★★★ Cathedral. Toledo's cathedral is considered the finest expression of the Gothic style in Spain. It was begun in 1226, completed at the end of the 15th century, and further embellished in succeeding centuries. Like many churches of the period, it was built over the great mosque, which once occupied the site. The cathedral is made of the palest stone, which seems to amplify the spacious interior, lit by 15th- and 16th-century **stained glass windows**. An enormous Gothic *retablo* dominates the **main altar**, theatrically lit by shafts of sunlight that enter through the cathedral's most extraordinary and unique feature, the ***Transparente***. This surprising Baroque concoction is a hole in the roof, around which stucco angels swirl. The **cloister**, with its lacy stonework, is quiet and contemplative. ⏱ *1 hr. Calle Cardenal Cisneros 1.* ☎ *925-22-22-41. www.architoledo.org. Admission (includes museum) 7€, free Sun afternoon. Mon–Sat 10am–6.30pm and Sun 2–6.30pm.*

4 ★★ Iglesia de Sant Tomé.
This was El Greco's parish church, and it has won its place on every tourist's itinerary thanks to a single painting: *The Burial of the Count of Orgaz*, which El Greco painted for the church between 1586 and 1588. This huge canvas updates a popular local story about the 14th-century knight Don Gonzalo Ruíz, a famously pious and philanthropic man whose

Toledo's Gothic Cathedral.

⑤ ★ Casa-Museo El Greco. It seems unlikely that El Greco actually lived in this attractively restored 16th-century mansion, but his home was probably very similar. The rooms are filled with period furniture, including some colorful ceramic tiles, and serve as a backdrop to a fine collection of the artist's work (I always particularly enjoy the scenes of Toledo, which remain surprisingly unchanged). *C/ Samuel Leví s/n.* ☎ *925-22-44-05. Currently closed for major restoration.*

⑥ ★ Sinagoga del Tránsito and Museo Sefardí. One of Toledo's trio of surviving synagogues is now an interesting museum dedicated to Jewish culture. The Jews were expelled from Spain in 1492, but previously Toledo had been home to one of the largest Jewish communities on the peninsula. The Sinagoga del Tránsito was built in the 13th century, with funds raised by Samuel Leví, financier to Pedro the Cruel (who eventually had Samuel tortured to death). The synagogue is a jewel of Mudéjar architecture, with a magnificent gilded ceiling and horseshoe arches. ⏱ *30 min. C/ Samuel Leví.* ☎ *925-22-36-65. www.museosefardi.net. Dec 8–Feb 14 Tues–Sat 10am–6pm, Feb 15–Dec 7 10am–9pm. Admission 2.40€, free on Sat afternoon and Sun.*

family would later become the Counts of Orgaz. It was said that at his funeral, Saints Stephen and Augustine descended from heaven to bury him with their own hands. In El Greco's version, the onlookers at the funeral (which include a self-portrait of the artist) are famously life-like portrayals of the notable men of Toledo at the time. ⏱ *30 min. Plaza del Conde 4.* ☎ *925-25-60-98. www.santotome.org. Admission 1.90€, free to Spanish citizens on Wed afternoon. June–Sept Mon–Sat 10am–7pm, Oct–May Mon–Sat 10am–6pm and Sun 10am–2pm.*

The decorated walls of the Sinagoga del Tránsito.

Practical Matters: Toledo

By car from Madrid, take the A-42 motorway to Toledo; the trip is 89km. Frequent Avant trains (journey time 30 mins, ☎ 902-24-02-02; www.renfe.es) leave from Madrid's Atocha station and arrive in Toledo, 2km from the old city center. **Oficinas de Turismo** are at Puerta de Bisagra (☎ 925-22-08-43) and Plaza del Consistorio 1 (☎ 925-25-40-30, www.toledo-turismo.org).

Lodging: Hotel La Posada de Manolo is a small, charming guesthouse (C/ Sixto Ramón Parro 8; ☎ 925-28-22-50; www.laposadademanolo.com; doubles 72–85€; MC, V). **Palacio Eugenia de Montijo** (Plaza Juego de Pelota 7; ☎ 925; www.hotel-palacioeugeniademontijo.com; doubles 120–180€) is a stylish boutique hotel with a tiny spa.

Dining: Adolfo Collection 1924 ($$) offers gourmet tapas and fine wines (C/ Nuncio Viejo, 1; ☎ 925-22-42-24). **Hostal del Cardenal** ($$$), in an 18th-century palacete, specializes in classic Castilian cuisine (Paseo de Recadero 24, ☎ 925-22-08-62).

⑦ ★ Sinagoga de Santa Maria la Blanca. The Sinagoga de Santa Maria la Blanca, built in the late 12th century, was also converted into a church after the expulsion of the Jews. Fortunately, its serene ranks of pale stucco horseshoe arches have been untouched through the centuries, and this remains one of my favorite places in the whole city. *🕐 30 min. C/ de los Reyes Católicos 4. ☎ 925-22-72-57. Admission 1.90€. Daily 10am–4pm.*

⑧ ★ Monasterio de San Juan de los Reyes. Another corner I love in this beautiful city is the historic cloister of the Monasterio de San Juan de los Reyes, particularly in spring when the orange trees are in bloom. *🕐 30 min. C/ de los Reyes Católicos 2. ☎ 925-22-38-02. www.sanjuandelosreyes.org. Admission 1.90€. Daily 10am–6pm, until 7pm in summer. ●*

Monasterio de San Juan de los Reyes.

The
Savvy Traveler

Before You Go

Government Tourist Offices

In the US: 666 Fifth Ave., 35th Floor, New York, NY 10103 (☎ 212/265-8822); 8383 Wilshire Blvd., Suite 960, Beverly Hills, CA 90211 (☎ 323/658-7195); 845 N. Michigan Ave., Suite 915E, Chicago, IL 60611 (☎ 312/642-1992); and 1221 Brickell Ave., Suite 1850, Miami, FL 33131 (☎ 305/358-1992). **In Canada:** 2 Bloor St. W., Suite 3402, Toronto, Ontario M4W 3E2, Canada (☎ 416/961-3131). **In the UK:** 79 New Cavendish St, 2nd Floor, London W1W 6XB (☎ 020/7317-2010).

The Best Times to Go

April to early June and **September to late October** are the best times to visit Madrid, when the sky is bright blue but the temperatures are moderate. In **May**, the best traditional festival takes place in honor of the city's patron saint, San Isidro. I love the city in **June**, when the flowers are blooming in the parks and the Madrileños take to the streets. In hot and sweaty **August**, much of the city shuts down as its citizens head for the beaches. Many shops and restaurants close for the entire month, so be sure to call in advance. However, this is also when some of the best traditional festivals are held, including La Paloma. **November** to **February** is surprisingly cold, but you'll have the city to yourself, and prices drop for hotels and airfares. The **Christmas** season in Madrid, beginning in early **December** and extending through the first week of **January**, is especially festive.

As Spain's capital, Madrid is a popular year-round destination. It is also a major international trade fair and conference destination throughout the year, so mid- to high-range hotels should be booked well in advance.

Festivals & Special Events

SPRING **Semana Santa (Easter Week)** is a relatively low-key festival in Madrid, compared with the great Andalucian cities, but is still celebrated with solemn processions. The Easter celebrations in **Toledo** are splendid, particularly on Holy Thursday and Good Friday. May 1 is **May Day**, or Labor Day, and the streets are full of marching trade-union members. **May 2 (Día de la Comunidad)** is a public holiday, in commemoration of the Madrileño uprising against Napoleonic troops on that date in 1808. It's celebrated with outdoor concerts and traditional dancing on the Plaza Dos de Mayo, and a military parade through the city center. The city's biggest festival, the **Fiesta de San Isidro**, a colorful and electrifying spectacle of traditional dance, street parties, concerts, and special events, takes place for two weeks around May 15. During **Corpus Christi**, which falls in either late May or early June, the streets of Toledo are carpeted in flowers and a glittering procession takes place in the heart of the old city.

SUMMER The **Fiesta de San Antonio de la Florida** (June 13) is a delightfully old-fashioned neighborhood festival, with bunting, street parties, and a pilgrimage to the saint's church, beautifully frescoed by Goya. During the **Noche de Sant Juan** (June 23), Madrid celebrates the summer solstice with fireworks and bonfires in the Parque del Retiro. There are numerous big music festivals held in June and July, including **Festimad** (usually June) and **Summercase** (usually July). The great summer cultural festival **Veranos de la Villa** (July–Aug) has everything from classical drama to contemporary dance at the city's

Useful Websites

www.okspain.org: Tourist Office of Spain official US site; it has detailed 'Before You Go' information (including US air departures).

www.spain.info: This comprehensive and high-tech website from the Spanish Tourist Office contains a wealth of information on everything from accommodation to museums.

www.munimadrid.es: Useful, city-run website with practical information on the city's main sights, parks, sports facilities, and more. In Spanish only.

www.renfe.es: The official site for Spanish rail travel, with routes, schedules, and booking. In Spanish only.

top venues. August is a wonderful month for *castizo* ('genuine') neighborhood festivals, held in honor of their patron saints: best of these is **La Paloma** (Aug 15) in La Latina, **San Lorenzo** in Lavapiés (Aug 10), and San Cayetano in Cascorro (Aug 7). Celebrations continue for about a week on either side of the saint's feast day. **Assumption Day** (Aug 15) is celebrated as a public holiday.

FALL The **Romería de Nuestra Señora Virgen de Gracia**, a pilgrimage that culminates in a huge group picnic, takes place in San Lorenzo de Escorial on the second Sunday of September. The **Noche Blanca** is a new cultural festival, with free events across the city during the night of September 23, from circus performances and music concerts to free access to museums.

WINTER **All Saints' Day** (November 1), a public holiday, is reverently celebrated: relatives and friends visit the graves of loved ones and eat traditional foods. Madrid has two patron saints: San Isidro, whose fiesta is celebrated in May, and the **Virgen de la Almudena** (November 9) whose feast day is marked with two weeks of festivities. The weeks leading to **Navidad**, or

Christmas, are marked by Christmas fairs in the Plaza Mayor (the largest), and several other squares throughout the historic center, selling handicrafts, Christmas decorations, trees, and Nativity figurines (for their *belenes*—nativity dioramas). The city council erects its own nativity scene in the Plaza de la Villa, in front of the city hall. **Día de los Reyes** (Three Kings Day), Jan 6, remains the traditional Catholic celebration of Christmas gift-giving (even though Santa Claus has made inroads and many families now exchange gifts on December 25). The evening before public celebrations take place in cities and towns across Spain; in Madrid, the main parade is led by three costumed Magi who parade through the Plaza Mayor throwing candy to children. **Carnaval** (just prior to Lent) in Madrid is low-key, with dressing up only by groups of children or stall owners in the local markets.

The Weather
Madrid is set on a high plateau in the center of Spain—which means searingly hot summers and bitterly cold winters. As a local saying goes, the capital endures 'nine months of winter and three months of hell'.

However, even the coldest days are usually sunny, with the beautiful bright blue skies immortalized in Goya's great paintings. Rain usually falls in short, but intense, thundery bursts, particularly in April and October, so come prepared. In July and August, the temperatures regularly soar well above 30°C (86°F), without a breath of wind to keep you cool. However, air-conditioned museums, restaurants, and hotels can keep the worst of the heat at bay. Copy the locals and retire to your room for a siesta, emerging once the worst of the heat has passed.

www.esmadrid.com: The city's official tourism site, in several languages, with flashy graphics and plenty of useful information for business and leisure travelers. Can be hard to find what you're looking for.

Cellphones (Móviles)

World phones—or GSM (Global System for Mobiles)—work in Spain (and most of the world). If your cellphone is on a GSM system, and you have a world-capable multiband phone, you can make and receive calls from Spain. Just call your wireless operator and ask for 'international roaming' to be activated. You can also rent a GSM phone. It may work out cheaper to simply buy a pay-as you-go phone once in Madrid. These are available from the department store **El Corte Inglés** (Calle Preciados 3, ☎ 91-379-80-00) and **FNAC** (Calle Preciados 28, ☎ 91-595-61-00) among others. You can usually buy a simple phone

for around 50€, which usually includes around 20€ of credit. It is also possible to buy a Spanish Sim card for your own phone, but check with your operator to ensure that your phone is unlocked. North Americans can rent a GSM phone before leaving home from **InTouch USA** (☎ 800/872-7626; www.intouchglobal.com) or **RoadPost** (☎ 888/290-1606 or 905/272-5665; www.roadpost.com).

Car Rentals

Driving in Madrid isn't advised, especially with the preponderance of inexpensive taxis and metro services. The day trips we have suggested are all easily accessible by public transport, although it is easier to combine visits (for example, visiting Aranjuez and Toledo in one day) if you rent a car. North America's biggest car-rental companies, including Avis, Budget, and Hertz, maintain offices in Madrid, including at Barajas airport and the Atocha and Chamartín rail stations. The best deals can usually be found on the Internet, so shop around before coming. Useful contact details include: **Avis** (☎ 800/331-1212; (US), ☎ 08445 818181 (UK), ☎ 902-135-531 (Spain); www.avis.com), **Hertz** (☎ 800/654-3131 (US), ☎ 08708 448844 (UK); www.hertz.com), and **Budget** (☎ 800/472-3325 (US), ☎ 08701 565656 (UK); www.budget.com). Spanish company **Pepecar** (☎ 807-41-42-43, www.pepecar.com) offers low-cost car rental in Madrid.

Getting **There**

By Plane

From Madrid's **Barajas** airport (12km from the city center), there are several ways to get into town.

The most convenient is the **metro** (line 8), with stations at Terminals 2 (also for Terminals 1 and 3) and 4. Single tickets cost 2€ (note that public transport passes require a supplement payment of 1€ for journeys to and from the airport). **Bus** services link the airport with the **Avenida de América** bus station in northeast Madrid (which is also on the metro network). Take bus no. 200 from Terminals 1, 2, and 3, and bus no. 204 from Terminal 4. Tickets cost 1€. Taxis leave from outside all terminals. A journey to the city center shouldn't cost more than 30€, including the airport and luggage supplements. Ask for a receipt.

By Car
Several major highways converge on Madrid, at the very center of Spain. Highway **A-2** leads to Zaragoza and Barcelona in the northeast, and the **A-3** heads directly east to Valencia. The **A-6** runs northwest towards Galicia (take this for Segovia and Ávila), and the **A-5** heads southwest towards Extremadura and Seville. The **A-42** is a direct highway to Toledo. The city is encircled by three major ring roads: the **M-30**, the **M-40**, and the **M-50**. Traffic is very sluggish, particularly during rush hour, when it regularly slows to a standstill.

By Train
Most national (RENFE: www.renfe.es) and international trains arrive at **Atocha**, Glorieta del Emperador Carlos V, (☎ 91-506-61-95; Metro: Atocha), or **Chamartín**, Calle Augustín de Foxa s/n, (☎ 91-323-15-15; Metro: Chamartín) in the north. **Atocha** is the biggest station in Spain, and the terminus of the AVE high-speed rail links with Barcelona and Seville.

Getting **Around**

By Metro
The **Metro** (☎ 902-44-44-03; www.metromadrid.es) is Madrid's efficient, modern, and clean subway. The extensive network (12 color-coded lines, plus the 'R' Ópera-to-Principe Pío link) makes it the fastest and easiest way to navigate the city. Red diamond symbols with a blue Metro sign mark stations. Single-ticket fares (sencillo) are 1€, although you can get a Metrobús pass (good for 10 trips on the metro or the bus) for 7€. This is usually better value than the tourist passes (abono turístico), which are valid for unlimited travel for periods of between 1 and 7 days (I day pass 5€, 2 days 8.40€, 3 days 11€, 5 days 16.80€, 7 days 22.60€, with a 50% discount for children under 11). The Metro runs daily 6am–2am, with fewer services on Sundays.

By Taxi
Taxis, which are white with a red diagonal stripe on the front doors, are plentiful and reasonably priced; few journeys cost more than 10€. You can either hail a cab in the street (the green light on the roof means it's available) or grab one where they're lined up (usually outside hotels). There are taxi ranks at the two main train stations, Atocha and Chamartín, and at several city center locations including the Plaza Isabel II and the Plaza Callao (on the Gran Vía). Taxi ranks are identified with a blue sign with the white letter 'T'. Fares begin at 1.95€ (2.15€ at night), with supplements for journeys to and from airport, rail, and bus stations. There is no supplement for luggage or the transport of wheelchairs. Note that if you order a taxi by phone, you will also pay for the time it takes to arrive at your

call-out point. Reliable taxi companies include **Radio Taxi** (☎ 91-447-51-80) and **Teletaxi** (☎ 91-371-21-31). **Euro Taxi** has specially adapted taxis for the disabled: book in advance (☎ 91-547-85-00).

By Bus

Buses are plentiful and convenient, but occasionally frustratingly slow because of the high volume of traffic on the city roads. On the plus side, they are refreshingly air-conditioned in summer. The night buses (called *búhos*, meaning owls) operate 11.15pm–5.10am. The *búhometro* is a relatively new nightbus service that follows the routes of the metro lines 12.45–5.45am. Single tickets for bus journeys, including night buses, cost 1€, although the Metrobús pass (see above) offers the best value.

By Car

Trying to negotiate Madrid's unfamiliar, traffic-clogged streets can be nerve-racking, and parking is an expensive nightmare. The day trips I've described here—Toledo, El Escorial, and Aranjuez—are all easy to reach by public transport. However, a car is useful if you plan to combine out of town day trips, or simply want to explore the surrounding countryside at your leisure.

On Foot

Strolling in central Madrid is a pastime verging on an art form, and the compact city is ideal for walking, especially in the atmospheric maze of the old center near the Plaza Mayor. The wide avenues of Salamanca may be shopping heaven, but it can be a bit of slog getting around this extensive neighborhood.

Fast **Facts**

APARTMENT RENTALS Among the options are: **Friendly Rentals** (☎ 93-268-80-51; www.friendly rentals.com), which has stylish properties at surprisingly good value; **www.spain-select.com**, which offers luxurious apartments in the city's smartest neighborhoods; and **www.rentmadrid.com**, with a choice of properties in the old center.

ATMS/CASHPOINTS Maestro, Cirrus, and Visa cards are readily accepted at all ATMs. Exchange currency at banks or *casas de cambio* (exchange houses). Banks usually offer the best deals, but *casas de cambio* are open later. They usually charge hefty commission rates, so check before you make any transactions. You can also find currency exchange offices at the Atocha rail station and Barajas airport. Spanish

banks include Caja de Madrid, BBVA, and Santander. Branches of these are located near the Plaza Mayor and along the Gran Vía. Most banks offer 24-hour ATMs: these are usually the best way to access local currency in Spain, but check rates with your own bank.

BUSINESS HOURS Banks are open Mon–Fri 8:30am–2pm. Most offices are open Mon–Fri from 9am to 6 or 7pm (in July, 8am–3pm). In August, businesses are on skeleton staff if not closed altogether. At restaurants, lunch is usually from 1:30 or 2 to 4pm and dinner 9–11:30pm or midnight. Major stores are open Mon–Sat from 9:30 or 10am to 8pm, with many stores in shopping malls also opening on the first Sunday of the month; staff at smaller establishments, however, often still close for siesta in the mid-afternoon, doing business from 9:30am–2pm and 4:30–8 or 8:30pm.

DOCTORS Dial ☎ **112** for any emergency, including medical emergencies. The old local number (used before the introduction of the Pan-European emergency number, 112), 061, is still valid. For information on local doctors, call the city information line 012.

ELECTRICITY Hotels operate on 220 volts AC. The El Corte Inglés department store (Calle Preciados 3, ☎ 91-379-80-00) has adaptors.

Embassies USA, Calle Serrano 75, in Salamanca (☎ 91-587-2303); **Canada**, Calle Núñez de Balboa 35 (☎ 91-423-32-50); **UK,** Calle Fernando el Santo 16 (☎ 91-700-82-00); **Australia**, Plaza del Descubridor Diego de Ordás 3 (☎ 91-353-66-00); **New Zealand**, Plaza de la Lealtad 2 (☎ 91-523-02-26).

EMERGENCIES For all emergencies, call the pan-European emergency telephone number ☎ **112**, although the old numbers still function: ☎ 061 for ambulance; for fire ☎ 080.

GAY & LESBIAN TRAVELERS In 1978, Spain legalized homosexuality among consenting adults, and in 1995, Spain banned discrimination based on sexual orientation. Marriage between same-sex couples became legal in 2005. Madrid is one of the major centers of gay life in Spain, with the vibrant neighborhood of Chueca the capital of the gay scene. You'll find shops, bars, restaurants, hotels, and more clustered in this area. Across the rest of the city, the gay scene is less visible than in other Spanish destinations, such as Barcelona or Sitges. The websites www.gayinspain.com and www.chueca.com have complete and destination-specific listings for gay travelers.

HOLIDAYS Holidays observed include: January 1 (New Year's Day), January 6 (Feast of the Epiphany), March 19 (Saint Joseph), Mar/Apr (Good Friday), May 1 (May Day), May 2 (Fiesta de la Comunidad), August 15 (Feast of the Assumption), October 12 (Spain's National Day), November 1 (All Saints' Day), December 6 (Constitution Day), December 8 (Feast of the Immaculate Conception), and December 25 (Christmas).

INSURANCE Check your existing insurance policies before you buy travel insurance to cover trip cancellation, lost luggage, medical expenses, or car rental insurance. For more information, contact one of the following recommended insurers: **Access America** (☎ 866/807-8300; www.accessamerica.com); **Travel Guard International** (☎ 800/826-4919; www.travelguard.com); **Travel Insured International** (☎ 800/243-3174; www.travelinsured.com); and **Travelex Insurance Services** (☎ 888/228-9792; www.travelex-insurance.com). For travel overseas, most US health plans (including Medicare and Medicaid) do not provide coverage, and the ones that do often require payment for services upfront. If you require additional medical insurance, try **MEDEX Assistance** (☎ 800/537-2029; www.medexassist.com) or **Travel Assistance International** (☎ 800/821-2828; www.travelassistance.com). For general information on services, call the company's Worldwide Assistance Services, Inc. (☎ 800/777-8710).

INTERNET Internet access is plentiful, both in cybercafés (*Internet cafés* or *cibercafés*) and frequently in hotels, several of which now offer WiFi. The **Café Comercial**, Glorieta Bilbao 7, ☎ 91-521-56-55, is old and atmospheric and has a couple of creaky terminals. There are numerous *locutorios* (phone centers) clustered around the Puerta del Sol, where you can make cheap international calls and usually get online at several terminals. **Easynet cafés** (Calle Alberto Aguilera 27, near the Argüelles metro, and Glorieta de Quevado 5, metro Quevado) are huge and cheap, if soulless. **Workcenter** (the branch at Plaza Canalejas is the most convenient; find more branches at www.work center.es) has a wide range of business and printing services, as well as fast Internet access.

LOST PROPERTY   Call credit card companies the minute you discover your wallet has been lost or stolen and file a report at the nearest police precinct. Your credit card company or insurer will almost certainly require a police report number or record. **Visa's** emergency number is ☎ 900-99-11-24 in Spain. **American Express** cardholders and traveler's check holders should call ☎ 902-37-56-37 in Spain. **MasterCard** holders should call ☎ 900-97-12-31 in Spain.

MAIL & POSTAGE   Spanish post offices are called *correos* (koh-*ray*-os), identified by yellow-and-white signs with a crown and the words *Correos y Telégrafos*. Main offices are generally open 9am–8pm Mon–Fri and Sat 9am–7pm. The Central Post Office is at Plaza Cibeles s/n, not too far from the Prado (☎ 91-523-06-94). Other branches are at Carrera de San Jerónimo s/n, Calle Alcalá 7–9, and Plaza Oriente s/n.

MONEY   The single European currency in Spain is the **euro.** At the time of going to press, the exchange rate was approximately 1€ = \$1.25 (or £0.84). For up-to-the minute exchange rates between the euro and the dollar, check the currency converter website **www.xe.com/ucc**.

PASSPORTS   No visas are required for US or Canadian visitors to Spain providing your stay does not exceed 90 days. Australian visitors do need a visa. If your passport is lost or stolen contact your country's embassy or consulate immediately. See 'Embassies' above. Make a copy of your passport's critical pages and keep it separate from your passport.

PHARMACIES   Pharmacies *(farmacias)* operate during normal business hours and one in every district remains open all night and on holidays. The location and phone number of this *farmacia de guardia* is posted on the door of all the other pharmacies. A couple of central pharmacies open 24/7 include **Farmacia de la Paloma**, Calle Toledo 46, ☎ 91-365-34-58, *www.farmacia delapaloma.com*, and **Farmacia del Globo**, Calle Atocha 46 (☎ 91-359-20-00).You can also call the city information line ☎ **012** for the addresses of all-night pharmacies.

POLICE   For all emergencies, call ☎ **112**. The old numbers (which existed prior to the introduction of the pan-European emergency number) still exist: national police ☎ 091 and local police ☎ 092.

SAFETY   Violent crime in Madrid is a rarity, but petty criminals frequent tourist areas and major attractions such as museums, restaurants, hotels, trains, train stations, airports, subways, and ATMs. Exercise care around major tourist sights, especially around the Plaza Mayor, the Gran Vía, and the neighborhoods of Lavapiés and La Latina. Be especially careful of pickpockets on the metro, and do not allow flower-bearing gypsies to approach you anywhere. Be equally careful of young women and children bearing clipboards with fake sponsorship forms: this is a common scam to pick your pockets. Do not enter any of the public parks after nightfall.

SATE (Servicio de Atención al Turista Extranjero) (Tourist Attention Service), Calle Leganitos 19, (☎ 91-548-85-37), has English-speaking attendants who can aid crime victims in reporting losses and obtaining new documents. The office is open 9am–10pm.

SMOKING   A law banning smoking in public places, including on public transportation and in offices and hospitals was enacted in early 2006. However, only larger bars and restaurants are forced to provide a non-smoking section, while smaller establishments are simply allowed to choose whether to become smoking or non-smoking. The few non-smoking bars (about 5%) have prominent signs. If you feel strongly about avoiding second-hand smoke, ask establishments if they have a *no fumadores* (non-smoking) section, or choose a restaurant with an outdoor terrace.

TAXES   The value-added (VAT) tax (known in Spain as *IVA*) ranges from 7% to 33%, depending on the commodity being sold. Food, wine, and basic necessities are taxed at 7%; most goods and services (including car rentals) at 13%; luxury items (jewelry, all tobacco, and imported liquors) at 33%; and hotels at 7%. Non EU residents are entitled to a reimbursement of the 16% IVA tax on most purchases worth more than 90€ made at shops offering 'Tax Free' or 'Global Refund' shopping. Forms, obtained from the store where you made your purchase, must be stamped at Customs upon departure. For more information see **www.globalrefund.com**.

TELEPHONES   For national telephone information, dial ☎ 11888. For international telephone information, call ☎ 11886. You can make international calls from booths identified with the word *Internacional*. To make an international call, dial

☎ 00, wait for the tone, and dial the country code, area code, and number. If you're making a local call, dial the two-digit city code first (**91** in Madrid) and then the seven-digit number. To make a long-distance call within Spain, the procedure is exactly the same because you must dial the city prefix no matter where you're calling.

TIPPING   More expensive restaurants add a 7% tax to the bill and cheaper ones incorporate it into their prices. This is *not* a service charge, and a tip of 5–10% is expected from tourists in these establishments, although locals rarely leave more than a couple of euros. For coffees and snacks most people just leave a few coins or round up to the nearest euro. Taxis do not expect tips, although they might hope for something from tourists. Tip hotel porters and doormen 1€ and maids about the same amount per day.

TOILETS   In Spain they're called *aseos*, *servicios*, or *lavabos*, and are labeled *señores*, *hombres*, or *caballeros* for men and *damas* or *señoras* for women.

TOURIST INFORMATION   **Turismo de Madrid**, Plaza Mayor 27 (☎ 91-588-16-36), is run by the city council and offers a wealth of information as well as useful maps and a free monthly magazine (*esMadridmagazine*) with excellent event listings. For information on the city plus the surrounding area (the Comunidad de Madrid) visit the **Oficina de Turismo de la Comunidad de Madrid**, Calle Duque de Medinaceli 2 (☎ 91-429-49-51). Tourism information offices are also at Atocha train station and the airport. Call ☎ 012 for general visitor information.

TRAVELERS WITH DISABILITIES   Much of Madrid is steep and even cobbled in some areas, making it awkward for wheelchair-users. Many of the older buildings in Madrid have stairs, making it difficult for visitors with disabilities to get around, though conditions are slowly improving. Newer hotels are more sensitive to the needs of persons with disabilities, and more expensive restaurants are generally wheelchair-accessible. The city tourism website, www.esmadrid.com, has lists of accessible museums, hotels, and shops, and also provides monthly updates on new services being introduced for disabled travelers. These include special guided tours, currently offered in Spanish only, but it is hoped that other languages will be introduced. (The website is not easy to navigate: go to 'Always', then click on 'Your Own Way', which brings up the Accessible Madrid option). You might consider taking an organized tour specifically designed to accommodate such travelers. In the US, **Flying Wheels Travel** (☎ 507-451-5005; www.flyingwheelstravel.com) sometimes offers escorted tours to

Spain, and **Access-Able Travel Source** (☎ 303-232-2979; www.access-able.com) has access information for people traveling to Madrid (as well as other worldwide destinations). Pick up a **metro** plan, which indicates stations with elevators and wheelchair access (also available at www.metromadrid.es). Most **buses** (www.emtmadrid.es) are equipped for wheelchairs, although it is advisable to travel off peak rather than fight your way through the crowds. All the sightseeing buses (Madrid Vision) can accommodate wheelchairs. **Famma**, Calle Galileo 69, www.famma.org, is a federation of private disabled organizations (☎ 91-593-35-50), which produces an excellent comprehensive guide (Spanish only) to accessibility in Madrid. It's currently being updated, but a version is available online. It includes accessibility appraisals of shops, hotels, theatres, and bus and train stations, among other institutions.

Madrid: **A Brief History**

C.1000 BC The first settlements in the Madrid area grow up along Manzanares river.

412 AD The Goths make Toledo their capital.

711 The Moors invade the Iberian peninsula.

C.860 The Arabic fortress of Mayrit (possibly the origins of the name 'Madrid') is established where the Royal Palace currently stands.

1083 Christian armies capture Madrid.

1202 Madrid is declared a free city in a statute issued by Alfonso VIII.

1309 The itinerant Spanish Cortes (parliament) is held in Madrid for the first time.

1202 Madrid is granted town status.

1492 Ferdinand and Isabella (the 'Catholic Monarchs') defeat Granada, the last Moorish kingdom on the Iberian peninsula. The Jews are expelled from Spain. Christopher Columbus reaches the Americas.

1495 A royal marriage unites the Spanish monarchs with the Austrian Habsburg Emperors.

1520 Castilian towns, including Madrid, join the *Comunero* revolt against Carlos I.

1561 Felipe II declares Madrid the first permanent capital of Spain. Numerous building projects are initiated.

1600–6 Madrid is briefly replaced by Valladolid as Spanish capital.

1620 Plaza Mayor is completed.

1700 Carlos II dies without an heir; Felipe V is crowned the first Bourbon king of Spain.

1701–13 Spanish War of Succession rips across the country.

1734 The Royal Palace is destroyed by a huge blaze.

1808 Napoleonic troops take Madrid, despite heroic resistance by the Madrileños. Carlos IV abdicates, and Napoleon appoints his brother Joseph as King of Spain.

1835 Mendizabel laws appropriate church property for the state.

1813 The Spanish monarchy is restored under Fernando VII.

1833–4 First Carlist Wars. Supporters of Isabel II defeat the pretender Don Carlos.

1868 General Prim declares the First Republic, triggering the Second Carlist War. Isabel II flees from Spain.

1876 Spanish monarchy once again restored to throne under Alfonso XII.

1908 Work begins on the Gran Vía.

1923 General Primo de Rivera declares his dictatorship, but is forced to resign six years later in the face of overwhelming economic problems.

1931 Spain votes overwhelmingly for a Republic and Alfonso XIII is forced to abdicate.

1936–9 Spanish Civil War. Madrid is the last city to fall to the Nationalists under Franco.

1975 Death of Franco and the coronation of Juan Carlos I.

1977 The Socialists win the first democratic elections in Spain since the Civil War. The following year, a new Spanish Constitution is signed.

1981 A right-wing military coup is foiled.

1980s The *Movida*, a socio-cultural movement that exploded across the city after the death of Franco, reaches its height. Alternative films, fashion, music, and art flourish.

1986 Spain joins the European Union.

1992 Madrid is European Capital of Culture.

1996 Conservative Partido Popular (PP) wins general elections.

2004 Terrorist attacks in Madrid claim the lives of 191 people. In the face of criticism over their handling of the crisis, the PP is ousted in General Elections and leader of the Spanish Socialist Party (PSOE) José Luis Rodríguez Zapatero becomes Prime Minister of Spain.

2005 The Reina Sofía is dramatically enlarged by Jean Nouvel.

2007 The Prado unveils its new extension by Rafael Moneo.

2008 Zapatero's Socialist government wins second term of office in general elections. A tragic plane accident at Barajas airport kills 154 people.

Madrid's **Architecture**

Moorish & Mudéjar (10th–13th C. AD)

Very few vestiges of the old Arabic citadel survive, besides a small stretch of the **old wall** in a shabby park near the Catedral de la Almudena. The Moors who converted and stayed behind after the Reconquest continued to work for their new Christian rulers, and their art, which fuses Arabic and European techniques, is called Mudéjar. The little Mudéjar church of **San Nicolás** preserves a minaret from the mosque that once occupied the spot, neatly capped and turned into a belltower. There are much finer examples of Mudéjar craftsmanship in Toledo, including the brilliant **Sinagoga del Tránsito**.

Gothic & Plateresque (15th–16th C.)

The best example of the Gothic style in the Madrid region (and one of the finest in all of Spain) is Toledo's majestic **cathedral**, with its pointed arches, elaborate sculptural decoration, and soaring vaults. Almost all the Gothic constructions in Madrid were destroyed, although the **Torre de los Lujanes** survives on the Plaza de la Villa. On this same square, the **Casa de Cisneros** features the delicate, intricate decorative stonework typical of Plateresque architecture, which derives its name from the *plateros* or silversmiths.

Renaissance & Baroque (16th–18th C.)

Madrid's Golden Age in terms of historic architecture was the 17th-century, when many of its most emblematic buildings were erected. The enormous palace at **El Escorial** is an elegantly restrained masterpiece by Juan Bautista de Toledo and his gifted collaborator Juan de Herrera, whose penchant for austere lines is echoed in the designs for the **Plaza Mayor**, completed in 1620 by one of his pupils. The **Monasterio de la Encarnación** and the **Monasterio de las Descalzes Reales** are both refined early-Baroque edifices, as is the **Casa de la Villa** (city hall). By the 18th-century, Baroque architecture was becoming more fulsome and lavish. Spanish monarchs invited Italian architects to design the new **Royal Palace**, which remains the city's largest and most opulent Baroque construction.

Neoclassicism, Eclecticism, Historicism (mid-18th– late-19th C.)

Under Carlos III and his Enlightenment ideals, the city was dramatically expanded and rebuilt. Architects sought inspiration in the cultures of Ancient Rome and Greece, adorning their buildings with classical columns and favoring straight, rational lines over the fanciful loops of Baroque. New projects included the majestic **Prado**, one of the first purpose-built museums in Europe, and the original hospital, which now contains the **Reina Sofía** museum. The pretty little **Observatory**, tucked away in a corner of the Retiro Park, is a jewel of Neoclassical architecture. The splendid **Cibeles fountain**, with its depiction of the ancient goddess in her chariot, is another fine example of Neoclassicism. Towards the end of the 19th-century, Neoclassicism began to merge with Eclecticism and Historicism as architects began to conflate different styles and influences in one building. The best examples of this type of architecture can be found in the first swathe of the **Gran Vía**, at the junction with Calle Alcalá, where buildings clearly inspired by the French Second Empire rub shoulders with restrained Neoclassical mansions.

Modern & Contemporary (early 20th c.–present)

The first buildings of the Gran Vía were erected in the first decade of the 20th century—grand, showy, and designed to demonstrate to the world that Madrid was a forward-thinking modern capital. This street, like no other, captures the architectural trends of the succeeding century. As the Gran Vía spreads slowly west, the buildings unfold in a textbook explanation of 20th-century Madrileño architecture. There are very few Art Nouveau (called Modernisme in Spain) buildings in the city, although the sublime **Sociedad de Autores**, just north of the Gran Vía, is a remarkable exception. However, Art Deco was extremely popular, inspired in part by the startling new skyscrapers mushrooming in the big North American cities. The Gran Vía boasts several sensuously curved, Art Deco monuments, including the **Edificio Carrión** and the **Palacio de la Prensa** on the Plaza del Callao. The Franco years saw virtually no modern architecture of note, apart from a couple of skyscrapers remarkable only for their height. Architecture was little better served in the post-Franco era, with a clutch of banks and business towers, such as the **Puerta de Europa**, a pair of skyscrapers leaning towards each other, which were completed in 1996. The greatest critical successes of the early 21st century have all been conversions to existing buildings. Rafael Moneo's glassy expansion of the **Prado** (2007), Jean Nouvel's striking new addition to the **Reina Sofía** (2005), and Herzog & De Meuron's clever conversion of a factory into the **CaixaForum** have all raised the city's artistic profile considerably.

Useful Phrases & Menu Terms

Useful Words & Phrases

ENGLISH	SPANISH	PRONUNCIATION
Good day	Buenos días	*bweh*-nohs *dee*-ahs
How are you?	¿Cómo está	*koh*-moh es-*tah*
Very well	Muy bien	mwee byehn
Thank you	Gracias	*grah*-thee-ahs
You're welcome	De nada	*deh nah*-dah
Goodbye	Adiós	ah-*dyos*
Please	Por favor	por fah-*vohr*
Yes	Sí	see
No	No	noh
Excuse me	Perdóneme	pehr-*doh*-neh-meh
Where is . . . ?	¿Dónde está . . . ?	*dohn*-deh es-*tah*
To the right	A la derecha	ah lah deh-*reh*-chah/
To the left	A la izquierda	ah lah ees-*kyehr*-dah
I would like . . .	Quisiera	kee-*syeh*-rah
I want . . .	Quiero	*kyeh*-roh
Do you have . . . ?	¿Tiene usted?	tyeh-neh oo-*sted*

English	Spanish	Pronunciation
How much is it?	¿Cuánto cuesta?	*kwahn*-toh *kwehs*-tah
When?	¿Cuándo?	*kwahn*-doh
What?	¿Qué?	Keh
There is (Is there. . . ?)	(¿)Hay (. . . ?)	aye/ee ah
What is there?	¿Qué hay?	keh aye
Yesterday	Ayer	ah-*yehr*
Today	Hoy	oy
Tomorrow	Mañana	mah-*nyah*-nah
Good		Bueno *bweh*-noh
Bad	Malo	*mah*-loh
Better (Best)	(Lo) Mejor	(loh) meh-*hohr*
More	Más	mahs
Less		Menos *meh*-nohs
Do you speak English?	¿Habla inglés?	*ah*-blah een-*glehs*
I speak a little Spanish	Hablo un poco de español	*ah*-bloh oon *poh*-koh deh es-pah-*nyol*
I don't understand	No entiendo	noh ehn-*tyehn*-doh
What time is it?	¿Qué hora es?	keh *oh*-rah ehss
The check, please	La cuenta, por favor	lah *kwehn*-tah pohr fah-*vohr*
the station	la estación	lah es-tah-*syohn*
a hotel	un hotel	oon oh-*tehl*
the market	el mercado	ehl mehr-*kah*-doh
a restaurant	un restaurante	oon rehs-tow-*rahn*-teh
the toilet	el baño	ehl *bah*-nyoh
a doctor	un médico	oon *meh*-dee-koh
the road to. . .	el camino a	ehl kah-*mee*-noh ah
to eat	comer	ko-*mehr*
a room	una habitación	*oo*-nah ah-bee-tah-*syohn*
a book	un libro	oon *lee*-broh
a dictionary	un diccionario	oon deek-syoh-*nah*-ryoh

Numbers

NUMBER	SPANISH	PRONUNCIATION
1	uno	(*oo*-noh)
2	dos	(dohs)
3	tres	(trehs)
4	cuatro	(*kwah*-troh)
5	cinco	(*theen*-koh)
6	seis	(says)
7	siete	(*syeh*-teh)
8	ocho	(*oh*-choh)
9	nueve	(*nweh*-beh)
10	diez	(dyehth)
11	once	(*ohn*-theh)
12	doce	(*doh*-theh)
13	trece	(*treh*-theh)
14	catorce	(kah-*tohr*-theh)

15	quince	(*keen*-seh)
16	dieciséis	(dyeh-thee-*says*)
17	diecisiete	(dyeh-thee-*syeh*-teh)
18	dieciocho	(dyeh-thee-*oh*-choh)
19	diecinueve	(dyeh-thee-*nweh*-beh)
20	veinte	(*bayn*-teh)
30	treinta	(*trayn*-tah)
40	cuarenta	(kwah-*rehn*-tah)
50	cincuenta	(theen-*kwehn*-tah)
60	sesenta	(seh-*sehn*-tah)
70	setenta	(seh-*tehn*-tah)
80	ochenta	(oh-*chehn*-tah)
90	noventa	(noh-*behn*-tah)
100	cien	(*thyehn*)

Meals & Courses

ENGLISH	SPANISH	PRONUNCIATION
Breakfast	**Desayuno**	deh-sah-*yoo*-noh
Lunch	**Almuerzo**	al-*mwehr*-thoh
Dinner	**Cena**	*theh*-nah
Meal	**Comida**	ko-*mee*-thah
Appetizers	**Entremeses**	en-treh-*meh*-sehs
Main course	**Primer plato**	*pree*-mehr *plah*-toh
Dessert	**Postre**	*pohs*-treh

Table Setting

ENGLISH	SPANISH	PRONUNCIATION
Glass	**Vaso**	*bah*-soh
	or **Copa**	*koh*-pah
Napkin	**Servilleta**	sehr-vi-*lye*-tah
Fork	**Tenedor**	teh-neh-*dor*
Knife	**Cuchillo**	koo-*chee*-lyoh
Spoon	**Cuchara**	koo-*chah*-rah
Bottle	**Botella**	boh-*teh*-lyah
Cup	**Taza**	*tah*-thah

Decoding the Menu

ENGLISH	SPANISH	PRONUNCIATION
Baked	**Al horno**	ahl *ohr*-noh
Boiled	**Hervido**	ehr-*vee*-thoh
Charcoal grilled	**A la brasa**	ah lah *brah*-sah
Fried	**Frito**	*free*-toh
Grilled	**A la plancha**	ah lah *plan*-chah
Rare	**Poco hecho**	*poh*-koh *eh*-choh
Medium	**Medio hecho**	*meh*-dyo *eh*-choh
Well done	**Muy hecho**	mwee *eh*-choh
Roasted	**Asado**	ah-*sah*-thoh
Sauce	**Salsa**	*sahl*-sah
Spicy	**Picante**	pee-*kahn*-te
Stew	**Estofado**	ess-toh-*fah*-doh

Dining Out

ENGLISH	SPANISH	PRONUNCIATION
Check/bill	**Cuenta**	*kwen*-tah
Waiter	**Camarero** *(masc.)*	kah-mah-*reh*-roh
	Camarera *(fem.)*	kah-mah-*reh*-rah

Beverages

ENGLISH	SPANISH	PRONUNCIATION
Beer	**Cerveza**	thehr-*veh*-thah
Coffee	**Café**	kah-*feh*
Milk	**Leche**	*leh*-cheh
Pitcher	**Jarra**	*hah*-rah
Tea	**Té**	teh
Water	**Agua**	*ah*-gwah
Wine	**Vino**	*bee*-noh
Red	**Tinto**	*teen*-toh
Rosé	**Rosado**	roh-*sah*-thoh
White	**Blanco**	blahn-*koh*
Wine list	**Carta de vinos**	*kahr*-tah deh *bee*-nohs

Meat, Sausages & Cold Cuts

ENGLISH	SPANISH	PRONUNCIATION
Beef	**Buey**	*bway*
Duck	**Pato**	*pah*-toh
Meat	**Carne**	*kahr*-neh
Chicken	**Pollo**	*po*-lyoh
Cold meat	**Fiambre**	*fyam*-breh
Cutlet	**Chuleta**	choo-*leh*-tah
Ham	**Jamón**	hah-*mohn*
Cooked ham	**Jamón York**	hah-*mohn* york
Cured ham	**Jamón Serrano**	hah-*mohn* seh-*rah*-noh
Lamb	**Cordero**	kohr-*deh*-roh
Kidneys	**Riñones**	ree-*nyoh*-nehs
Liver	**Hígado**	*ee*-gah-thoh
Partridge	**Perdiz**	*pehr*-deeth
Pheasant	**Faisán**	fahy-*thahn*
Pork	**Cerdo**	*thehr*-doh
Rabbit	**Conejo**	koh-*neh*-hoh
Ribs	**Costilla**	kos-*tee*-lyah
Sausage	**Salchicha**	sahl-*chee*-chah
Spicy sausage	**Chorizo**	choh-*ree*-thoh
Steak	**Bistec**	*bee*-stehk
Sirloin	**Solomillo**	so-loh-*mee*-lyoh
Tripe	**Callos**	*kah*-lyohs
Turkey	**Pavo**	*pah*-voh
Veal	**Ternera**	tehr-*neh*-rah

Seafood & Shellfish

ENGLISH	SPANISH	PRONUNCIATION
Anchovy		
salt	Anchoa	ahn-*choh*-ah
fresh	Boquerón	boh-*keh*-rohn
Bass	Lubina	loo-*bee*-nah
Bream (porgy)	Besugo	beh-*soo*-goh
Cod	Bacalao	bah-kah-*lah*-oh
Crab	Cangrejo	kan-*greh*-hoh
Crayfish	Cigala	see-*gah*-lah
Cuttlefish	Jibia	*hih*-byah
Fish	Pescado	pess-*kah*-thoh
Flounder	Platija	plah-*tee*-hah
Hake	Merluza	mehr-*loo*-thah
Grouper	Mero	*meh*-roh
Lobster	Langosta	lahn-*goss*-tah
Mackerel	Caballa	cah-*ba*-lyah
Monkfish	Rape	*rah*-peh
Mussel	Mejillón	meh-hee-*lyohn*
Octopus	Pulpo	*pool*-poh
Oyster	Ostra	*ohs*-trah
Prawn	Gamba	*gahm*-bah
Red mullet	Salmonete	sal-moh-*neh*-teh
Salmon	Salmón	sal-*mohn*
Sardine	Sardina	sahr-*dee*-nah
Scallop	Peregrina	peh-reh-*gree*-nah
Shellfish	Mariscos	mah-*reess*-kohs
Sole	Lenguado	len-*gwah*-tho
Shrimp	Camarón	ka-mah-*rohn*
Squid	Calamar	kah-lah-*mahr*
Swordfish	Pez espada	*peth* ess-*pah*-thah
Trout	Trucha	*troo*-chah
Tuna	Atún	ah-*toon*
Turbot	Rodaballo	roh-dah-*ba*-lyoh

Vegetables & Legumes

ENGLISH	SPANISH	PRONUNCIATION
Carrot	Zanahoria	thah-nah-*oh*-ryah
Cabbage	Col	kohl
Red cabbage	Lombarda	lom-*bahr*-dah
Celery	Apio	*ah*-pyoh
Chickpea	Garbanzo	gahr-*bahn*-thoh
Corn	Maíz	mah-*eeth*
Eggplant	Berengena	beh-rehn-*jeh*-nah
Fava (broad) beans	Habas	*ah*-bahs
Green beans	Judías	hoo-*dee*-yahs
Lentil	Lenteja	lehn-*teh*-hah
Leek	Puerro	*pweh*-roh
Lettuce	Lechuga	leh-*choo*-gah
Mushroom	Seta	*seh*-tah

The Savvy Traveler

ENGLISH	SPANISH	PRONUNCIATION
Potato	**Patata**	pah-*tah*-tah
Pumpkin	**Calabacín**	kah-lah-bah-*theen*
Salad	**Ensalada**	enn-sah-*lah*-dah
Spinach	**Espinaca**	ess-pee-*nah*-kah
Onion	**Cebolla**	theh-*bo*-lyah
Tomato	**Tomate**	toh-*mah*-teh
Vegetables	**Verduras**	vehr-*doo*-rahs

Miscellaneous

ENGLISH	SPANISH	PRONUNCIATION
Banana	**Plátano**	*plah*-tah-noh
Bread	**Pan**	pahn
Bread roll	**Bollo**	*bo*-lyoh
Butter	**Mantequilla**	mahn-teh-*kee*-lyah
Caramel custard	**Flan**	flahn
Cheese	**Queso**	*keh*-soh
Egg	**Huevo**	*weh*-boh
Fruit	**Fruta**	*froo*-tah
Ice cream	**Helado**	eh-*lah*-doh
Omelet	**Tortilla**	tohr-*tee*-lya
Pepper	**Pimienta**	pee-*myen*-tah
Rice	**Arroz**	*ah*-rohth
Salt	**Sal**	sahl
Sugar	**Azúcar**	ah-*thoo*-kahr

Toll-Free Numbers & Websites

AER LINGUS
☎ 800/474-7424 in the U.S.
☎ 01/886-8844 in Ireland
www.aerlingus.com

AIR CANADA
☎ 888/247-2262
www.aircanada.ca

AIR FRANCE
☎ 800/237-2747 in the U.S.
☎ 0820-820-820 in France
www.airfrance.com

AIR NEW ZEALAND
☎ 800/262-1234 or -2468 in the U.S.
☎ 800/663-5494 in Canada

☎ 0800/737-000 in New Zealand
www.airnewzealand.com

ALITALIA
☎ 800/223-5730 in the U.S.
☎ 8488-65641 in Italy
www.alitalia.it

AMERICAN AIRLINES
☎ 800/433-7300
www.aa.com

AUSTRIAN AIRLINES
☎ 800/843-0002 in the U.S.
☎ 43/(0)5-1789 in Austria
www.aua.com

BMI
No U.S. number
☎ 0870/6070-222 in Britain
www.flybmi.com

BRITISH AIRWAYS
☎ 800/247-9297 in the U.S.
☎ 0870/850-9-850 in Britain
www.british-airways.com

CONTINENTAL AIRLINES
☎ 800/525-0280
www.continental.com

DELTA AIR LINES
☎ 800/221-1212
www.delta.com

EASYJET
No U.S. number
www.easyjet.com

IBERIA
☎ *800/772-4642 in the U.S.*
☎ *902/400-500 in Spain*
www.iberia.com

ICELANDAIR
☎ *800/223-5500 in the U.S.*
☎ *354/50-50-100 in Iceland*
www.icelandair.is

KLM
☎ *800/374-7747 in the U.S.*
☎ *020/4-747-747 in the Netherlands*
www.klm.nl

LUFTHANSA
☎ *800/645-3880 in the U.S.*
☎ *49/(0)-180-5-838426 in Germany*
www.lufthansa.com

NORTHWEST AIRLINES
☎ *800/225-2525*
www.nwa.com

QANTAS
☎ *800/227-4500 in the U.S.*
☎ *612/131313 in Australia*
www.qantas.com

SCANDINAVIAN AIRLINES
☎ *800/221-2350 in the U.S.*
☎ *0070/727-727 in Sweden*
☎ *70/10-20-00 in Denmark*
☎ *358/(0)20-386-000 in Finland*
☎ *815/200-400 in Norway*
www.scandinavian.net

SWISS INTERNATIONAL AIRLINES
☎ *877/359-7947 in the U.S.*
☎ *0848/85-2000 in Switzerland*
www.swiss.com

UNITED AIRLINES
☎ *800/241-6522*
www.united.com

US AIRWAYS
☎ *800/428-4322*
www.usairways.com

VIRGIN ATLANTIC AIRWAYS
☎ *800/862-8621 in continental U.S.*
☎ *0870/380-2007 in Britain*
www.virgin-atlantic.com

Photo **Credits**

day BY day

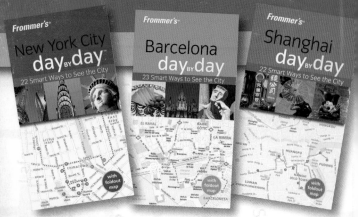

Get the best of a city in 1,2 or 3 days

Day by Day Destinations

Europe

Amsterdam
Athens
Barcelona
Berlin
Bordeaux &
   Southwest France
Brussels & Bruges
Budapest
Edinburgh
Dublin
Florence and Tuscany
Lisbon
London
Madrid
Malta & Gozo
Moscow
Paris
Provence & the Riviera

Prague
Rome
Seville
St Petersburg
Stockholm
Valencia
Vienna
Venice

**Canada and The
Americas**

Boston
Cancun & the Yucatan
Chicago
Honolulu & Oahu

Los Angeles
Las Vegas
Maui
Montreal
Napa & Sonama
New York City
San Diego
San Francisco
Seattle
Washington

Rest of the World

Beijing
Hong Kong

Frommer's®

...anded Imprint of ⓦWILEY

Avail... ...oks are sold